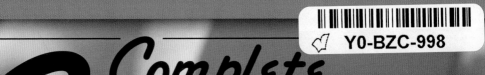

# Complete Guitar

hinkler

*Simply Guitar* is dedicated to Ian and Dianne MacKay (Mum and Dad)
for everything they have done for me.

Special thanks to Metropolis Audio (Simply Guitar)

Published by Hinkler Books Pty Ltd
45–55 Fairchild Street
Heatherton Victoria 3202 Australia
www.hinkler.com.au

hinkler

Author: Steve MacKay
Cover Design: Sam Grimmer
Internal Design: Ruth Comey and Sam Grimmer
Typesetting: MPS Limited (Lead Guitar)
Photography: Ned Meldrum
Prepress: Graphic Print Group

ISBN: 978 1 7418 3619 6

Printed and bound in China

# CONTENTS

# Lead Guitar . . . . . . . . . . . . . . . . . . . . . . . . . . . . . 67

# SIMPLY
# GUITAR

# INTRODUCTION

The Simply Guitar section has been written for those of you who may have never played guitar and feel a little intimidated by it, and those of you who already play, but need some of the gaps in your knowledge and technique bridged before you can progress any further.

I have taught students of all ages and skill levels and I find the same questions keep recurring:
'It seems like there are at least a million notes on the guitar ... How am I supposed to learn and remember them? How do I get my fingers to do what I tell them to do? What do all these fancy terminologies mean? What is that chord and how do I play it? Why don't the songs I'm trying to play sound like they should? Why does my guitar sound like a box with elastic bands on it?'

The first thing we have to get straight before we begin is that playing guitar is not a walk in the park. It takes hard work, dedication to practise and a love of music to get any results. Reading this section and following the DVD should open a few doors, but it is up to you to walk through them.

Like learning almost anything new, it can be as difficult or as simple as you want it to be, or as difficult or as simple as the teacher makes it. If you currently have a guitar teacher and you feel learning guitar is an impossible feat, either ask for the explanations to be simplified or get a new guitar teacher!

After reading this section and watching the DVD you should:

• Understand the ins and outs and dos and don'ts of guitar.

• Know the names of the strings.

• Know how to find all the notes on the guitar.

• Know what chords are and how to play them.

• Know how chords are formed.

• Know how to read and write tablature.

• Be able to play through chord progressions with relative ease.

Above all, I hope you would have gained a deeper understanding of what guitar is, how you can move forward with it as a creative and expressive tool and, most importantly, how to have fun with it!

# How to Purchase Your First Guitar

There are a lot of misconceptions about buying a guitar. People tend to bypass the less aesthetically pleasing or second-hand guitars for the cheaper, shiny-looking brand new ones that come with the free leopard-skin strap. As hard as it is to understand, the cool looking guitars aren't always the best to play. So how do you know what is good and what is unsuitable?

After years of buying the wrong guitars and learning the hard way, I've found there are two golden rules:

1 Spend as much money as your budget will allow. You get what you pay for.

2 Whenever you buy a guitar, you must have it SET UP! Then from that point on, have it set up at least once a year. I cannot stress the importance of this enough. When you buy a car, you don't drive it until it falls apart – you have it serviced. Guitars are the same.

## So what is a set-up and where do I get one?

With the right expert (expert being the operative word), a set-up can turn what seems like a hopeless piece of firewood into a nice playable guitar. You wouldn't go to a butcher to get your appendix out, so make sure you don't take your guitar to Bob over the back fence who has a new screwdriver set. Make some enquires in music stores and, even better, ask any working guitarist. The aim is to go with the most reputable person you can.

## When you're in the store, what should you look for?

*Does it feel good to hold?*
Sit down on a chair (preferably with no arms) and hold the guitar as you would if you were going to play it. If you are holding it correctly, it should mould to your body and you shouldn't feel any discomfort.

*What is the action like?*
The 'action' is the distance between the strings and the fret board. Ideally, a nice low action is the best for a number of reasons, the main reason being it makes playing guitar easier!

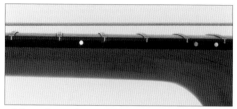

**High Action**: The distance between the strings and the fret board is quite substantial. This makes it uncomfortable and difficult to press the fingers down on notes. WARNING: High action will impair your ability to progress on the guitar if not fixed with a set-up!

**Low Action**: The distance between the strings and the fret board is slight but they do not actually touch. This makes pressing the fingers down on notes more comfortable and easier. WARNING: If the action is too low, the strings will buzz on the frets and affect the sound of the guitar. A good way to tell if this is happening is to play every single note on the guitar with one finger. If it sounds nice and clean,

there's no problem. If there are strange buzzes and inconsistencies in the sound, the action is set too low. This can also be remedied by a good set-up.

*Does it stay in tune?*
Playing an out-of-tune guitar is like eating your breakfast cereal with bat milk. I've never done it, but I'm sure it doesn't taste right! Make sure the guitar is tuned before you test it, and then when it is tuned, play it solidly for around 5 minutes. If it stays in tune, great. If it is out of tune, it could be fixed with a set-up, but if you can't find a guitar that stays in tune after 5 minutes of playing, I'd probably go to another guitar store! If you can't play yet, ask the person selling it to tune it and then demonstrate the guitar for you – no stairway to heaven!

# KNOW YOUR INSTRUMENT

It is imperative to study the following two pages so that you know your instrument. Understanding what part or component of the guitar is being referred to when you read this book, watch the DVD or invest in any other instructional information is a big advantage and will avoid confusion about terminology.

## ACOUSTIC GUITAR

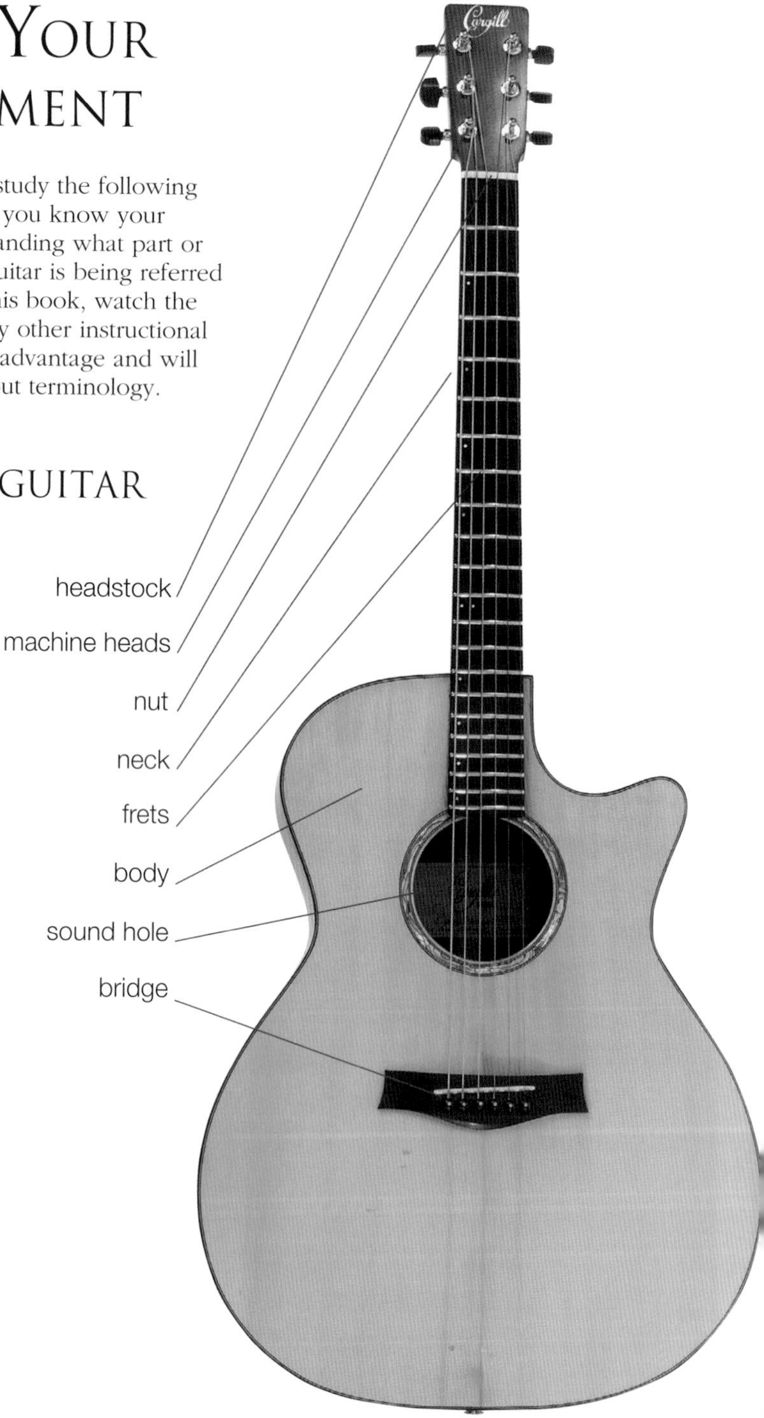

headstock

machine heads

nut

neck

frets

body

sound hole

bridge

# ELECTRIC GUITAR

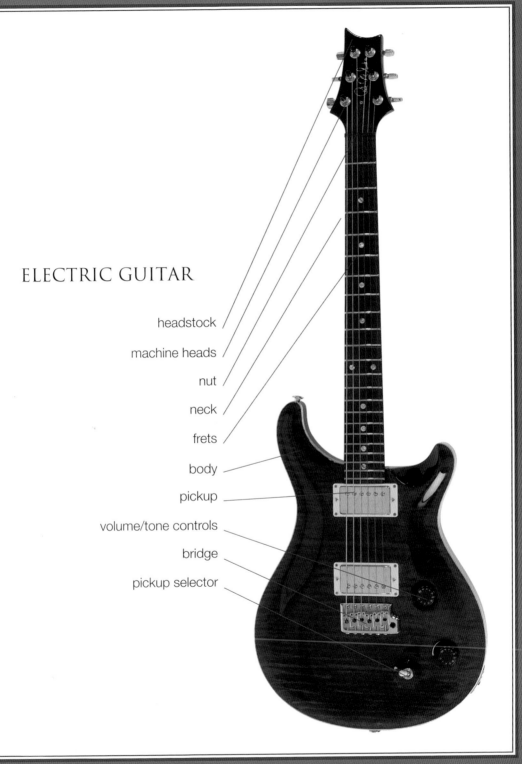

headstock

machine heads

nut

neck

frets

body

pickup

volume/tone controls

bridge

pickup selector

# WHAT YOU NEED

It would be great for the development of your playing and practice to try to purchase the following items, which are available from any good music store. Don't be afraid to ask for a demonstration!

## Metronome
Metronomes keep time for you, either by beeping or ticking to a tempo (speed) and time signature (amount of beats) that you set manually.

## Electronic guitar tuner
Tuners make tuning the guitar an easy task. They have a simple needle or light that indicates when the string is in tune.

## Pitch pipe
A great little tool if you are tuning your guitar by ear. Using a pitch pipe will give you a reference pitch to tune one string. You then tune the remaining strings from the string tuned to the reference pitch.

## Assortment of plectrums
Plectrums are those little things you see people strumming and picking the guitar with. Plectrums (or picks) come in all shapes and sizes. I recommend Jim Dunlop Jazz III picks or anything above 1mm thick (for a softer sound experiment with softer picks).

## String winder
A nifty device created to speed up the process of winding on new strings.

## Capo
A capo is a clamp that you place across all six strings to alter the pitch of the guitar.

## Good stool or armless chair
It seems simple, but if you're going to be playing guitar a lot, make sure you have a comfortable chair or stool with no arms, as arms can get in the way of holding the instrument correctly or can damage the guitar.

## Music stand
A music stand is great because it enables you to shorten the distance between what you're reading and your left hand (right hand if you are left handed).

# CORRECT POSTURE

It is possible to get back, neck, arm, hand and finger injuries from holding the guitar with incorrect posture. The most important thing to remember is that you should never be tense or in pain – always remember to relax!

Notice how the guitar shape is usually designed with the human body in mind. The curvature of the guitar body allows the guitar to sit comfortably on your thigh, and the neck is scaled so that your left arm (right arm if you are left handed) is free to move up and down the guitar with ease.

### How your left hand should be positioned
(right if you are left handed)

Have your thumb centred on the back of the guitar neck and relatively straight (back view). Your fingers should be curved and straight. This creates what is commonly referred to as 'the claw' grip, with the second and third fingers touching the thumb (the claw). We will cover specifics later in the book, but in the meantime try and emulate these pictures to the best of your ability.

### Holding a plectrum (pick)

The first three step-by-step pictures demonstrate how to hold the plectrum. The fourth picture is simply a different view of the third picture, taken from underneath the hand as opposed to above it.

1. Put your hand out as if you are going to do a karate chop
2. Bend your index finger inward as far as it will go comfortably
3. Sit the plectrum in between the outside of your index finger and your thumb

The plectrum should look as though it is coming out of the side of your thumb. The remaining fingers should be outstretched and relaxed. The pressure you apply to the plectrum should be minimal – try not to tense up when you play!

# How to Learn What and Where the Notes Are

First things first – what are the names of the strings? There is a lot of 'stuff' to remember when you start learning a new instrument. I find the best way to commit seemingly random ideas to memory is to create some sort of connection between what you are learning with something you already know, or that you could easily memorise. The best way to do this is by remembering by association. For example, the names of the strings on the guitar (from the thinnest to thickest) are E, B, G, D, A and E. There is no pattern or logic to the order, so make an acronym:

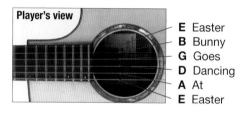

| | |
|---|---|
| **E** | Easter |
| **B** | Bunny |
| **G** | Goes |
| **D** | Dancing |
| **A** | At |
| **E** | Easter |

*How many notes are there in the musical alphabet?*

There are 7 NATURAL notes in Western music! They are: **A B C D E F G**

You may have noticed that the musical alphabet is identical to the normal alphabet, only it stops at G. Keep in mind, these are not all the notes in music. There are also sharps (that look like this – #) and flats (that look like this – b). What follows is an explanation to give you an understanding of how sharps and flats relate to natural notes:

**Ab** (flat)    **A** (natural)    **A#** (sharp)

Ab is one fret back from A natural.
A# is one fret forward from A natural.

This may come as a surprise for the less musically-inclined folks reading this but in total, there are only 12 notes in Western music! Here they are:

**A   Bb/A#   B   C   Db/C#   D**

**Eb/D#   E   F   Gb/F#   G   Ab/G#**

Notice how Bb (for example) can also be called A#. Whether you use sharps or flats is dictated by what key the music you are playing is in. This is a topic you don't have to worry about just yet.

It is extremely helpful if you can memorise the musical alphabet. To make things easier, you don't have to memorise the flats. We will only deal with the sharps for the time being. Referring back to what I said about turning things into acronyms or sayings earlier, the easiest way to memorise the musical alphabet is to identify what is different from the regular alphabet pattern we all know.

Here are a couple of suggested ways to remember this:

• Every note has a sharp after it except "BE"

• There is no B# and no E#

Run through this until you know it as well as you know your own name (it'll come in handy very soon!).

# KNOW ALL THE NOTES

## Neck perspective

There are many different ways of looking at the guitar when you play. You can look at the neck in chunks, diagonally, up and down, randomly and countless other ways. I suggest looking at it by the neck, string by string and horizontally, starting from the 1st fret all the way up to the 12th fret, almost like you have 6 keyboards lined up in front of you.

Now is a good time to mention the importance of reviewing everything slowly and carefully to ensure you have a good grasp on what is being taught.

## Learning all the notes

Now that you have the right perspective and can look at the neck in a simple way, all you need to do is apply everything you have learned so far (string names and musical alphabet) and develop your ability to navigate around the neck.

1. Play an OPEN A string (open means no fingers pressing down on the fret board).
2. Now put your first finger on the first fret. That note is A#.

3. Move up one more fret. That note is B.
4. Move up one more fret. That note is C.

Recognise the pattern?

| A | A# | B | C | C# | D | D# | E | F |
|---|----|---|---|----|---|----|---|---|

| F# | G | G# |
|----|---|----|

This same technique can be applied to all of the strings. Say you start on the OPEN D string. Now put your first finger on the first fret. That note is D#. Move up one more fret. That note is E, and so on.

| A | A# | B | C | C# | D | D# | E | F |
|---|----|---|---|----|---|----|---|---|

| F# | G | G# |
|----|---|----|

Now that you know the names of the strings, the musical alphabet and how to join the two together and navigate your way around the neck, all you have to do is become quicker and more proficient at doing so. The more you do something, the less you need to consciously think about it. Eventually you will be able to look at the neck and just see the notes.

### Tip:
Memorise the notes that fall on the dots. By doing this, you have more points of reference to figure out other unknown notes using the musical alphabet.

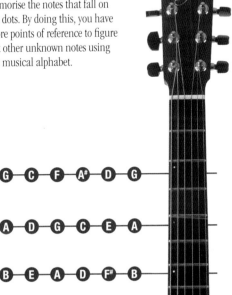

# POSITION PLAYING AND PLAYING 'IN POSITION'

Position playing is quite a simple concept that is designed to help the student understand the correct fingering of any particular music, be it a song, scale or chord.

*If I were to be in 1st position, it would mean:*

1st finger is on the 1st fret, 2nd finger is on the 2nd fret, 3rd finger is on the 3rd fret, 4th finger is on the 4th fret

*If I were to be in 5th position it would mean:*

1st finger is on the 5th fret, 2nd finger is on the 6th fret, 3rd finger is on the 7th fret, 4th finger is on the 8th fret

If this fret was the 9th fret, and your fingers were lined up exactly like this only starting from the 9th fret onwards, you would be in '9th position', and so on.

When in position, generally speaking, no finger should move from its designated fret. There are a number of reasons why you would want to implement position guidelines:

- To make playing the song easier and more fluent.
- Correct technique (traditionally there is a right and a wrong technique and bad habits are hard to break!).
- You have more than one finger so use them!

# Understanding Common Guitar Diagrams

There are two main types of diagrams that you will encounter when playing the guitar.

## Chord diagrams

These are pictures of the guitar neck with relevant information about which fret and what fingers to use. (A chord is more than one note played together at the same time – usually a minimum of three notes.)

- Chord diagrams are upright pictures of the guitar neck.

- The numbers represent which fingers you should use.

- The 'X' means don't play this string. The 'O' means play the string open.

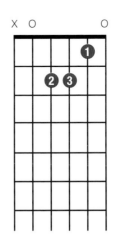

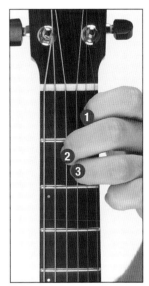

## Tablature

This is a visual guide showing where to put your fingers.

- Tablature is the easiest way to communicate music notation on the guitar.

- The lines represent the strings.

- The numbers represent the fret numbers you press on with your fingers.

- Sometimes a second set of smaller numbers is written underneath the fret numbers. These numbers would tell you which finger to use.

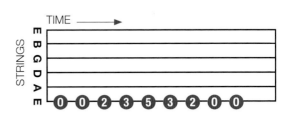

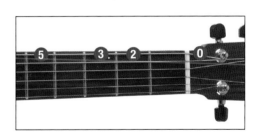

# TUNING THE GUITAR

The two most common ways to tune a guitar are:

1. Using a digital guitar tuner
2. By ear

The harsh reality about tuning a guitar by ear is that some people are tone deaf and can't tell if something is in tune or not. You do need an ear for music to know if the notes that you are playing together are in tune. In saying that, nobody usually starts tuning perfectly straight away. It takes practice, like anything else does.

The first thing you need to do when you are tuning your guitar by ear is to either assume the first string is relatively in tune, and tune the other strings from that, or tune the strings to the corresponding reference pitch from a keyboard or pitch pipe.

**Tuning the guitar, assuming the first string is in tune**

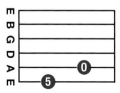

Play these two notes after each other

Because you have assumed the first string is in tune, you will only have to adjust the tuning key for the second string, matching what you hear from the reference pitch on the first string.

Is what you hear higher (sharper) or lower (flatter) to our reference pitch on the first string? Hopefully your guitar is strung properly, so that if you turn the tuning key for the second string anti-clockwise, the pitch will get higher, and if you turn the tuning key clockwise, the pitch will get lower.

NOTE: To know if your guitar has been strung properly refer to this picture. All your strings should wrap around the machine heads from the inside out, like so.

- From this point, you need to ascertain whether the second string sounds higher or lower compared to your reference pitch on the first string, then turn the tuning key clockwise or anti-clockwise accordingly.

- The notes should sound identical.

- When a string is out of tune you can usually hear a 'wow-wow' type of effect when you play it against your reference pitch.

OUT OF TUNE

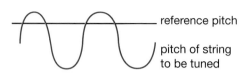

reference pitch

pitch of string to be tuned

IN TUNE

reference pitch

pitch of tuned string

When you feel you have the second string sounding identical to the reference pitch on the first string, the second string now becomes the reference pitch for the third string, and so on and so on.

To make sure you are getting the hang of this, let's go through tuning the third string to the reference pitch on the second string.

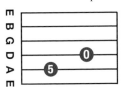
Play these two notes after each other

Is what you hear higher (sharper) or lower (flatter) than our reference pitch on the second string?

- From this point, you need to ascertain whether the second string sounds higher or lower compared to your reference pitch on the first string, then turn the tuning key clockwise or anti-clockwise accordingly.

- The notes should sound identical.

- When a string is out of tune you can usually hear a 'wow-wow' type of effect when you play it against your reference pitch.

Here are all the reference pitch notes for tuning the whole guitar in this fashion.

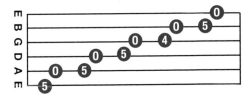

NOTE: This section on tuning can be very confusing, so don't worry if you don't quite get it when you read it. After watching the DVD and reading the section, you will really have a better understanding of how tuning works.

# TECHNIQUE FUNDAMENTALS

I think one of the most important attributes a student of guitar can have is the ability to identify where they are going wrong with their technique, in order to put into practice what to do right. Here are a few basic 'rules' to follow.

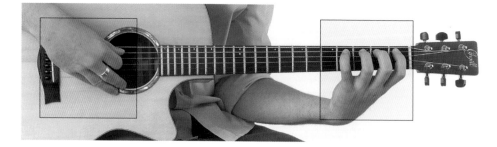

## RIGHT HAND RULES (pick technique)

- Fingers anchored to the body of the guitar
- Correct grip on the pick
- Alternate picking (down, up, down, up)

## LEFT HAND RULES

- Tips of fingers
- Fingers middle of the frets
- Curved fingers
- Straight claw-like hand shape
- Position playing
- Thumb in the middle of the neck

Now that you know what you are supposed to do, you really have to implement it in your playing with zero tolerance for deviation. In other words, no matter what you are playing, even if it is 'Mary Had A Little Lamb', aim to get every note played perfectly and aim to get your technique as flawless as you possibly can. Teaching yourself this way of practice will eventually lead you to do it naturally, and you will progress ten times faster than someone who practises without taking notice of what they are actually doing.

## Alternate picking

This part is very important to those of you out there who want to be able to play guitar at light speed (and shred like an 80s metal god!). For everyone else, it is important to learn the correct picking technique in order to play notes and chords with more ease. This is a hard lesson to learn if you have already been playing with a plectrum and haven't been alternate picking.

The idea is quite simple – when you pick down, pick up afterwards, regardless of whether you are changing strings or staying on the one string. The reason for doing so is to save time and make things easy on yourself. 'What goes down, must come up!'

Picking down          Picking up

Tap your foot! When ever you play guitar, tap your foot! It is as important as anything written on this page!

# THE CATERPILLAR

For a beginner, this exercise can be the guitar equivalent of a headache and endless re-runs of your worst nightmare! No, it's not that bad really. Just remember, no pain, no gain! The great thing I have found about the ol' 'Caterpillar' is that if it is practised daily and with the technique fundamentals outlined on the previous page, it can really accelerate your playing ability substantially.

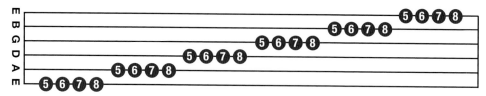

As you can see by the tablature above, it looks quite simple, but here's the trick:

1. Play each note without removing any of your fingers until they are needed to play another note.

2. Keep all of your fingers down so that you only move one finger at a time.

3. If you hear a buzz, or an inconsistency in the sound, or forget to implement the rules outlined on page 20, START OVER!

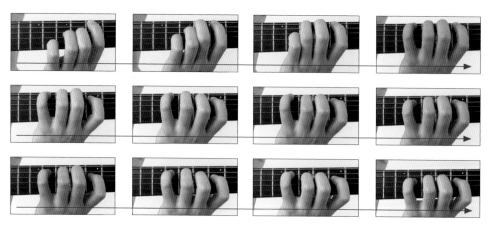

Repeat these steps until you can play through this exercise ten times at a slow pace without any mistakes. Do this religiously at least two minutes a day, then gradually increase the pace at a rate you can handle.

Now apply the same method to the next three strings, and remember, if you make a mistake, slow down and start from the beginning until you find a speed that enables you to run through the Caterpillar perfectly.

# BASIC CHORDS

These two pages cover all the basic major and minor chord shapes in alphabetical order. You will notice some chords are missing because they are more complicated and harder to play (we will get to those later in the book).

## BASIC MAJOR CHORDS

### A major
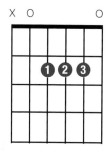

### C major
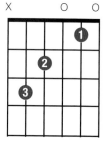

### D major
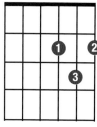

### E major
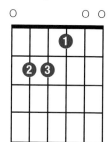

### G major
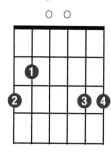

Major chords are happy sounding chords.

Go through and play each chord from this page and the previous page, one after the other, saying the name of the chord out loud as you play it. It is very important that you know what you are playing, and by reinforcing the chord names verbally to yourself you can more easily commit them to memory.

## BASIC MINOR CHORDS

### A minor

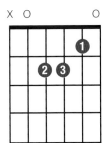 

### D minor

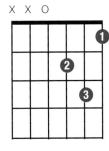 

### E minor

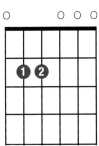 

Minor chords are sad sounding chords.

# Basic Chord Progressions

Now that you have learned the basic chords and memorized their shapes and names, it's time to put them into practice. Chord progressions are basically chords put into an order that works sonically, like a song!

You can experiment with strumming these chords any way you like at this stage. The aim is just to get the hang of playing through each chord to the next; we will cover strumming concepts a little later in the book. Run through each of these chord progressions, saying each chord's name as you play it.

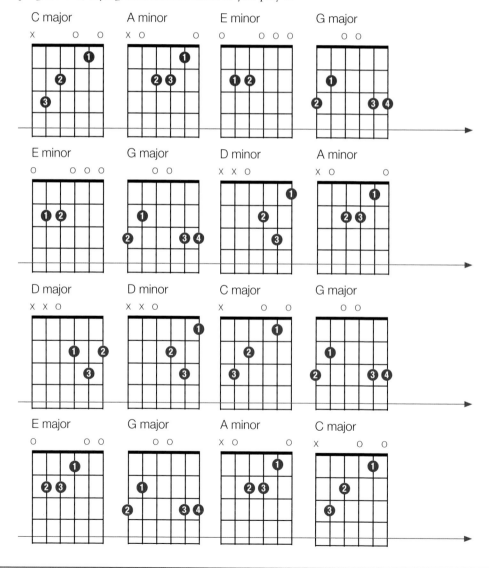

# Chord to Chord Transition Exercises

Now that you have learned the basic major and minor chords and played through a few progressions, it's time to make things smoother and easier. The secret to changing chords seamlessly and comfortably is training your fingers to move from chord to chord with minimal movement and visualising the transition.

Most people who learn chords and then start playing through progressions (songs) often play one chord, then completely remove all their fingers to form the next chord, so you end up hearing a chord then a gap while the next chord is being put into place.

I'm sure you could probably relate to what I am saying after your first attempt at playing through a chord progression fluently. It's harder than it looks, right?

So to get you heading in the right direction, let's break down the first chord progression on the previous page step by step (watch the DVD for a demonstration about putting this theory into practice).

Let's start with the C major chord to the A minor chord.

- Lift ONLY your third finger from the 3rd fret, A string
- Place it on the 2nd fret, G string without moving any other fingers
- Now you are playing A minor

Now the A minor chord to the E minor chord.

- Lift your first finger from the 1st fret, B string
- Prepare to place it on the 2nd fret, A string
- At the same time, remove your third finger from the 2nd fret, G string altogether

- Now implement the above instructions in one 'pivoting' movement
- You are now playing the E minor chord

Now the E minor chord to the G major chord.

- Lift your second finger from the 2nd fret, D string
- Prepare to place it on the 3rd fret, low E string
- At the same time, prepare to place your fourth finger on the 3rd fret, high E string and your third finger on the 3rd fret, B string
- Now implement the above instructions in one 'pivoting' movement
- You are now playing the G major chord

It sounds a little more complicated to read than it does to watch, so make sure you follow up this page by watching the corresponding section on the DVD.

Play through all of the chord progressions on page 26, strumming each chord 4 times – down then up, down then up (change chord), down then up, down then up, and so on.

Practise this strumming technique, implementing the chord transition ideas you have just learned, until each chord flows smoothly into the next and what you are playing is in time and actually sounds like a song.

We will talk about more in-depth strumming patterns a little later in the book, so make sure you have mastered it!

# How Chords Are Built and How to Build Them

The next piece of information could sound a little confusing at first, so try and go over it slowly and repeat it to yourself out loud.

Ok, here we go! All chords are made up from formulas. These formulas are simply combinations of notes from the major scale. Another way of looking at it would be pretending chords are cakes.

I know that sounds weird! So to clarify:

- Major scale = Supermarket (has all of the ingredients)
- Formula = Recipe (a combination of the ingredients)
- Chord = Cake (type of cake determined by what the ingredients are)

So far, you have played all the 'simple chords' (chords that have open strings), but you haven't touched on the major scale or formulas yet. So let's start with the major scale.

G major scale

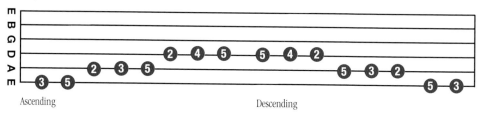

This particular major scale is a G major scale because the starting note is G and it is played in 2nd position.

If I play the exact same shape in 4th position, the starting note will be A and it will be the A major scale.

A major scale

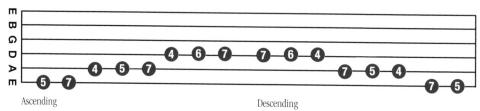

By memorising the 'shape' or the 'pattern' of the scale and moving it to any starting note on the low E string (or A string), you will have that note's major scale. Movable shapes are shapes you can move around!

# What You Need To Know About The Major Scale

**I**f you've seen 'The Sound of Music', you've heard the major scale. In fact, it is the most commonly used scale in Western music, and chances are you probably have it solidly embedded in your subconscious from singing nursery rhymes as a kid.

We could go on about the origins and oddities of the major scale but at this point it's safe to say you now know what the major scale is and what chords are, so now we just need cover this 'formula' business.

Formulas are made up of numbers. Those numbers represent notes in the major scale. Now when you play the MAJOR SCALE, number each note 1 to 8 starting from the start like so:

G major scale

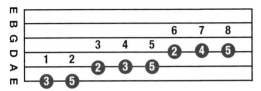

If you play 1 and 8 together you might recognise the shape known as an 'octave'. Octopus, octagon – eight. An octave is the 1st note and the 8th note of the major scale played together.

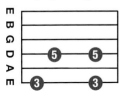

Two fret numbers placed on top of each other means 'play at the same time'.

For the punk rockers, if you play the 1st and the 5th notes together from the major scale, you might recognise the shape known as a 'power chord', or sometimes referred to as a '5th chord' (1st note and 5th note).

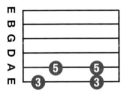

There are working guitarists out there that get away with just playing this one shape but in different positions, so you are almost ready to take on the world!

# CHORD FORMULAS

- Every major chord is made up of 1, 3, 5.
  The 1st note, 3rd note and 5th note of the major scale.

- Every minor chord is made up of 1, b3, 5.
  The 1st note, 3rd note flattened and 5th note of the major scale.

AHHHH! What does 3rd note flattened mean?
   I knew you would ask that one – refer back to our musical alphabet on page 14. To 'flatten' a note basically means to take it back one step. So if the 3rd is B, the flattened 3rd will be Bb.

To reinforce the whole formula idea, let's dissect the C major chord. First we need the numbered notes to the C major scale.

Now let's circle the formula 1, 3, 5.

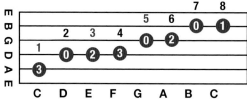

C major scale

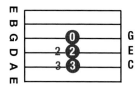

So in order to play a C major chord we need to play the C, E and G notes together somehow. We have four fingers and a thumb to use and six strings. Obviously you cannot play two notes on one string at the same time, so you have to find a way to play those notes together.

Here is the easiest way to play those notes:

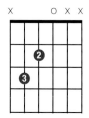

But we still have one finger and three strings left! What happens now? As long as you are playing the correct notes as stipulated in the formula (1st C, 3rd E, 5th G), all you need to do is repeat any of them until you have utilised the strings and the fingers you have left!

Here is the easiest way to do that. Find the choices you have.

Arrange your fingers and utilise the open strings according to the formula and the choices you have figured out.

 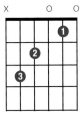

Notice this shape? That's right, it is the good ol' C major chord shape from page 24. Now you know why these chords are called 'basic chord shapes'. Once upon a time somebody figured out that these shapes are the easiest way to represent the formulas needed to construct the major and minor chords!

So hopefully your mind is ticking over with the possibilities. There are only 12 notes in music and 11 different ways to play them on the guitar (six strings, around 22 frets). You have four fingers and a thumb to use and you only need to play the 1st, 3rd and 5th notes of the major scale to form a major chord – there must be hundreds of ways to do the same thing? Yep, welcome to the infinite world of guitar!

If you're feeling ready, here are some other formulas for different types of chords to experiment with:

• Suspended 2nd (sus 2) = 1, 2, 5
• Suspended 4th (sus 4)  = 1, 4, 5
(Notice with 'sus' chords you always suspend the 3rd and replace with either a 2nd or a 4th)

Try and revise this section as much as possible, so that all this new information can sink in and start making some sense!

# TEST YOURSELF

## 20 QUESTIONS

This page is designed to test how much information has sunk in so far! Get yourself a blank piece of paper and write down the answers to the following 20 questions. Do not read the answers straight out of the book; you must be able to write the answers in your own words!

1. What does getting your guitar set up mean?
2. What is the action on a guitar?
3. What is considered to be good action?
4. What is a fret?
5. What is a fret board?
6. What are tuning keys and what do they do?
7. What is the claw?
8. Explain position playing.
9. What are the strings' names?
10. What is the musical alphabet?
11. How do you find notes on the guitar neck?
12. What is the note called on the 13th fret of the B string?
13. What is tablature?
14. What does a chord diagram look like?
15. What is a plectrum?
16. What do plectrums also get called?
17. What is alternate picking?
18. What is a chord progression?
19. What is a chord transition?
20. How do you build a D minor chord?

## 20 ANSWERS!

1. The answer can be found on page 8.
2. The answer can be found on page 8.
3. The answer can be found on page 8.
4. The answer can be found on page 10.
5. The answer can be found on page 10.
6. The answer can be found on page 10, 11, and 18.
7. The answer can be found on page 13 and 20.
8. The answer can be found on page 16.
9. The answer can be found on page 14.
10. The answer can be found on page 14.
11. The answer can be found on page 15.
12. C
13. The answer can be found on page 17.
14. The answer can be found on page 17.
15. The answer can be found on page 12.
16. The answer can be found on page 12.
17. The answer can be found on page 20.
18. The answer can be found on page 26.
19. The answer can be found on page 27.
20. Take the 1st, flattened 3rd and 5th notes of the D major scale and arrange them into a shape that works.

# PUTTING THE GROOVE INTO YOUR STRUMMING

If you have learned how to play through the chord progressions outlined on page 26 using the chord transition ideas covered on page 27, it's time to put some 'groove' into the equation!

Groove is extremely important; it can breathe life into what you play and helps the listener connect with what you are putting across. Groove will come naturally for some of you and harder for others – regardless which of the two you are, here are a few tips to get you started!

The way I think of putting groove into strumming is to look at the guitar strings like a drum kit.

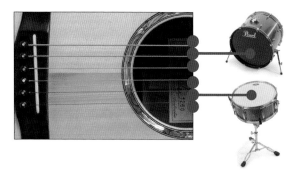

- The first three thick strings represent the **BASS** drum.

- The last three thin strings represent the **SNARE** drum.

Now think of the beat to 'We Will Rock You' by Queen.
BASS, BASS, SNARE . . . BASS, BASS, SNARE

TIME

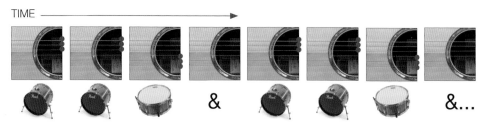

You can apply this theory to any chord progression and inject whatever feel you're capable of imagining into it! Experiment with the feel of the chord progressions you learnt on page 26.

Remember, it is very important to tap your foot when you play the guitar. It gives you a beat to be guided by and improves your general musicality; I cannot recommend tapping your foot enough!

# READING CHORD PROGRESSIONS WITH COUNTING

Counting can be a great help in mastering basic chord strumming grooves. Let's look at a few common strumming grooves and break them down with counting.

Let's simplify the explanations to make reading these grooves less confusing:

**D** = DOWN strum     **U** = UP strum     **B** = BASS drum     **S** = SNARE drum

| D/B | | D/S | | | | D/B | D/S | |
|---|---|---|---|---|---|---|---|---|
| **1** | & | **2** | & | 3 | **&** | **4** | &... | |

Okay, now we will make the groove spread out over 8 beats and include up strums:

| D/B | | D/B | | D/S | | | U/S | D/B | U/S | D/B | | D/S | | | U/S |
|---|---|---|---|---|---|---|---|---|---|---|---|---|---|---|---|
| **1** | & | **2** | & | **3** | & | 4 | **&** | **5** | **&** | **6** | & | **7** | & | 8 | **&** |

Always vocalise what you are playing. It's a great way to determine if you are doing it correctly or not.

Now let's get really tricky! We will practise playing a chord progression in a 3 feel (3 beats instead of 4).

| C<br>D/B | | C<br>D/B | | C<br>D/S | | Am<br>D/B | | Am<br>D/B | | Am<br>D/S | |
|---|---|---|---|---|---|---|---|---|---|---|---|
| **1** | & | **2** | & | **3** | & | **1** | & | **2** | & | **3** | & |

| Em<br>D/B | | Em<br>D/B | | Em<br>D/S | | G<br>D/B | | G<br>D/B | | G<br>D/S | |
|---|---|---|---|---|---|---|---|---|---|---|---|
| **1** | & | **2** | & | **3** | & | **1** | & | **2** | & | **3** | & |

Try and memorise these 3 strumming grooves until you feel you have mastered them. At this point you should have a good grasp of strumming down and up and knowing what to listen for when learning new songs with chord progressions.

# BARRE CHORDS

Now it's time to learn the missing chords from your chord artillery – barre chords! This is what I would consider to be your first real obstacle to overcome as a beginner to the guitar.

Here is a diagram of the main 4 barre chord shapes you will come across (check out the DVD for more info about this).

### E major shape barre

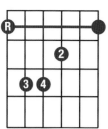 

### E minor shape barre

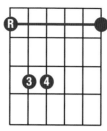 

### A major shape barre

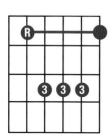 

### A minor shape barre

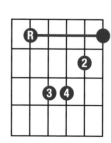 

I have labelled the 'root note'. The 'root note' is basically the note that gives the chord its name. For example: G major is 'G' major because the root note is G.

You might notice how I have named the barre shapes: E shape, Em shape, A shape and Am shape. That is because those chords are contained within the barre chords.

# HOW TO PLAY BARRE CHORDS

Here are a few things to think about while playing barre chords. The first is to realise that the index finger doesn't have to cover every note. For E shaped barre chords, it is only the low E string, B string and high E string that need to be covered. If you can learn to angle your index finger so that the point of direct contact and strength is over those strings, then your finger can still remain relatively relaxed. Keep in mind the pressure from your thumb on the back of the neck can be used as leverage for your index finger, which is doing the barring.

I find when I play barre chords, the point of contact on my index finger is the left hand side, with the palm facing upwards.

Another important thing to refer back to is our left hand rules and guidelines on page 20 (right hand if you are left handed). You should have a claw-like grip, with the thumb placed in the middle of the neck and (very importantly) straight – not off to the side or bent, as this will affect how your wrist and arm sits. You should not feel stress or pain whilst playing barre chords, although almost everyone does!

Looking at the diagrams, you will notice that the index finger 'bars' across the whole fret, and the remaining fingers form either an E, Em, A or Am shape. Playing what these diagrams show makes you realise the importance of good action!

# How to Use Barre Chords

The great thing about barre chords is that they are movable shapes. There's that movable word again, and it makes life easier! You just have to move the specific barre chord shape (E, Em, A, Am) to where you want on the neck, and you've got it! So let's go through a few together.

I want to form a B major barre chord starting on the low E string:

• Using the musical alphabet, I will have to figure out where B is on the E string.
• Then, when I realise it is on the 7th fret, I will barre my index finger on the 7th fret and form the E major shape with my remaining fingers (hopefully in one pivoting movement – the band won't wait for me to make my barre chord shape!).

Now I want to play a B major barre chord starting on the low A string:

• Using the musical alphabet, I'll figure out where B is on the A string.
• When I realise it is on the 2nd fret, I'll barre my index finger on the second fret and form the A major shape with my remaining fingers.

Notice any connections? E shape barre chords are for the E string (major and minor).
A shape barre chords are for the A string (major and minor).

Alternatively, if you make a barre chord on the neck and want to know what it is called:

• Ascertain whether it is major or minor by the shape (E, Em, A, Am).
• Find the root note (first note you play).
• Use your string name and musical alphabet knowledge to figure out the name of the root note.
• Voila! That's your barre chord!

# Moving On

If you have practised and learned everything from the previous pages, you've done extremely well. Congratulations! Now it's time to move on and discover some more complicated techniques, chords and theories.

Make sure you revise often and vocalise what you have learned while you practise it. It might make you feel crazy but I find if you cannot explain what you are doing, you don't really know, do you?

# FINGER STYLE PLAYING

I feel it is vital to be adept at finger style and plectrum playing to be a good all-around guitarist. In this chapter we will go through using all of your fingers, some finger style patterns and playing through chord progressions.

I find there are two main finger style positions that I use, the first one more so than the other. Here it is:

• The thumb controls the E, A and D strings while the index, 2nd and 3rd fingers control the G, B and E strings.

Note: In the second main position, the thumb controls the E and A strings while the index, 2nd, 3rd and 4th fingers control the D, G, B, E string.

Your thumb should be in front of your other fingers and your hand should stay relatively still. I find while I'm using the first finger style, I tend to anchor my little finger to the guitar. Doing this ensures that your hand remains still.

# FINGER STYLE PATTERNS

Here are 8 different finger style patterns using the chord progressions learned on page 26. Notice how the tab is more for the right hand, as the chords are indicated above the tab which the left hand plays. This type of tab will generally not deviate from the confines of the specific chords written above.

• The **small numbers** indicate which fingers to use on the RIGHT HAND. **T** indicates thumb.

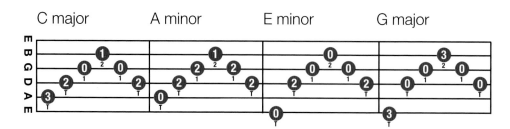

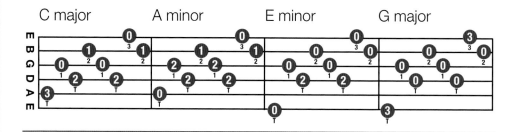

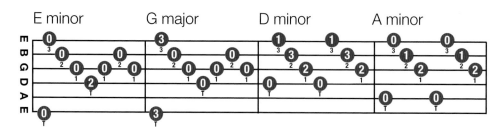

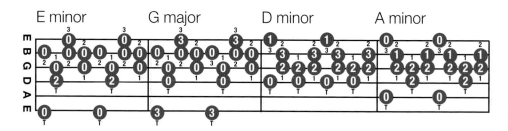

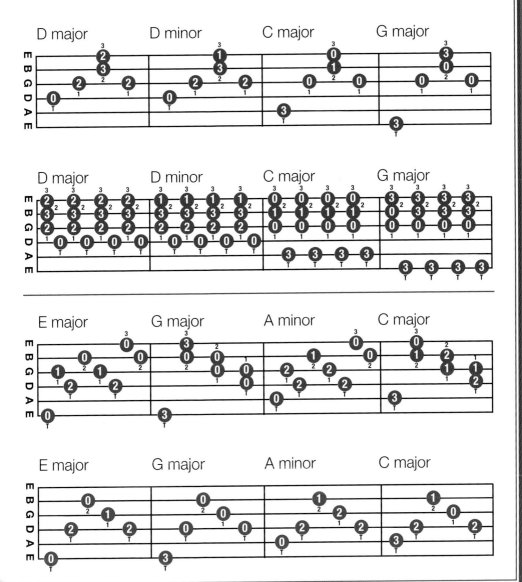

# ADVANCED CHORDS

The next two pages teach four new chords which I believe are important to have in your chord 'vocabulary'. Some shapes have open strings and other shapes are barred so it may appear a little inconsistent if you are like me and like things all neat and tidy! Aim to learn as many as you can and really take a good look at the shapes.

• Minor 7 (min7) • Dominant 7 (dom7) • Suspended 2nd (sus2) • Suspended 4th (sus4)

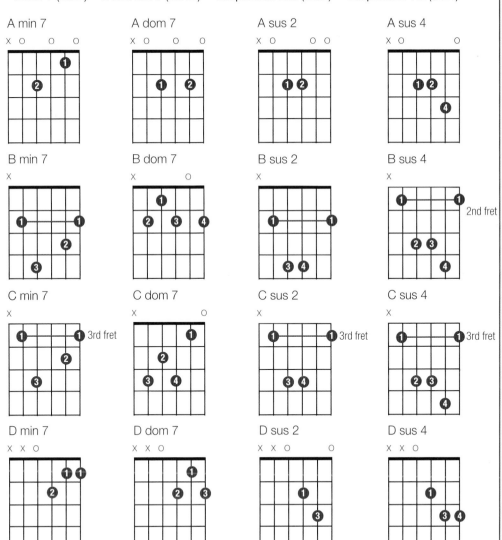

# ADVANCED CHORDS

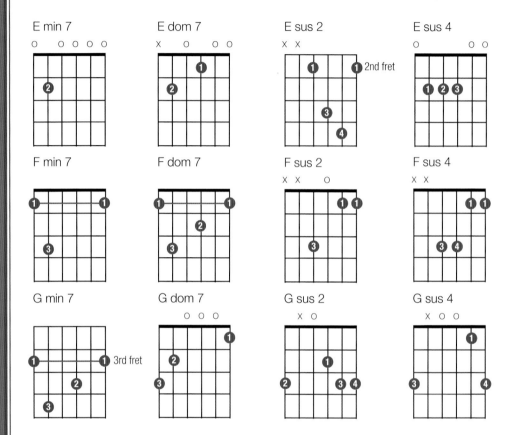

On the last two pages I have written out the min7, dom7, sus2 and sus4 shapes in alphabetical order, featuring the basic shapes whenever possible. Just remember that some of the shapes are barre shapes, because there are no commonly used basic shapes for that particular chord.

# Advanced Chords

On this page I will include just the movable barre shapes for the min7, dom7 and sus2 chords.

Min 7 (E Min 7 shape)

Dom 7 (E Dom 7 shape)

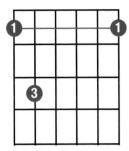
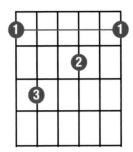

Min 7 (A Min 7 shape)
X

Dom 7 (A Dom 7 shape)
X

Sus 2 (A Sus 2 shape)
X

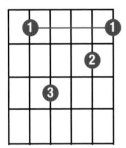
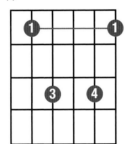
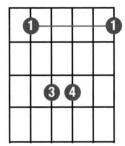

As you will notice with barre chords, the most commonly used shapes are either E or A shape based, as we discussed on page 36. For the record, you can actually turn all the basic chord shapes into barre shapes by following the same process as mentioned on page 36, but using alternate chords to the E and A shapes outlined. As you may have figured out, playing chords can be as in-depth or as simple as you want it to be!

# CHORD FINDER

Here are some handy chord shapes to have at your disposal.

To find A# / Bb, C# / Db, D# / Eb, F# / Gb, G# / Ab chord shapes, simply locate the appropriate chord types marked 'movable' and move them to where you want! Remember, the first note is the 'root' note (note that gives the chord its name).

# A

### A maj
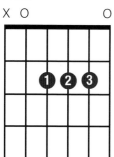

### A 7
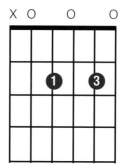

### A min
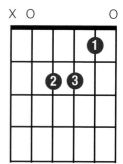

### A min 7
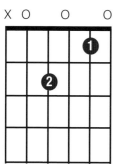

### A maj 7
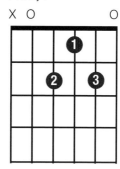

### A maj 7 b5
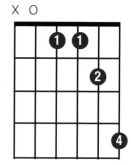

### A sus 2
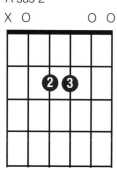

### A sus 4
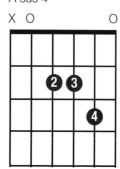

### A7 sus 4
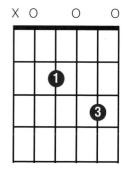

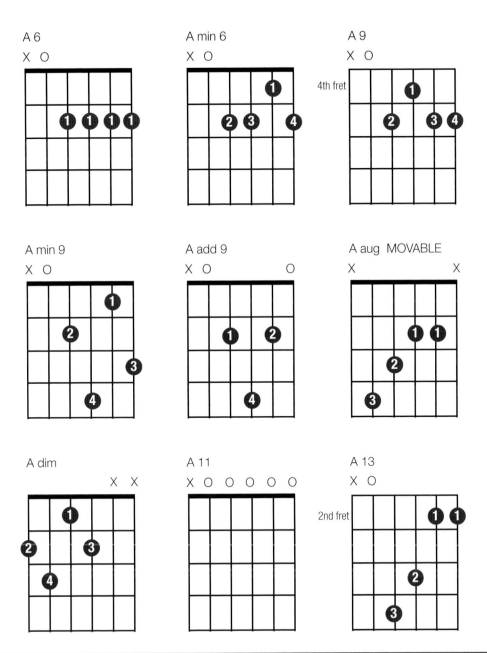

A 6

A min 6

A 9

A min 9

A add 9

A aug  MOVABLE

A dim

A 11

A 13

# B

### B maj  MOVABLE
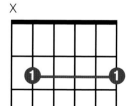

### B 7
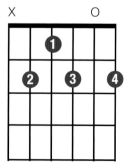

### B min  MOVABLE
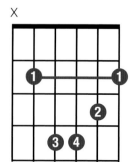

### B min 7  MOVABLE
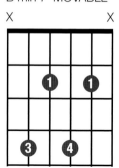

### B maj 7  MOVABLE
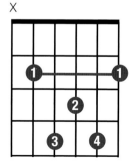

### B maj 7 b5  MOVABLE
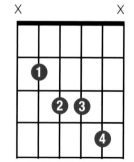

### B sus 2  MOVABLE
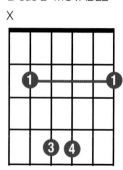

### B sus 4  MOVABLE
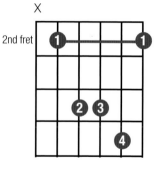

### B 7 sus 4
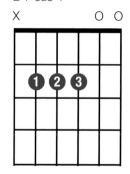

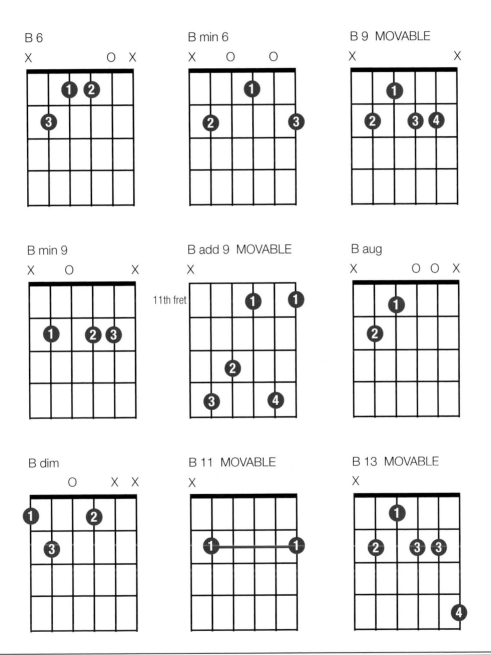

B 6

B min 6

B 9  MOVABLE

B min 9

B add 9  MOVABLE

11th fret

B aug

B dim

B 11  MOVABLE

B 13  MOVABLE

# C

### C maj

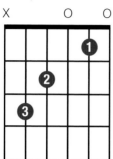

### C 7

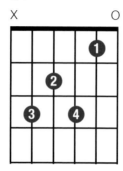

### C min

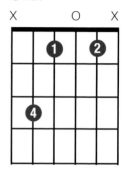

### C min 7  MOVABLE

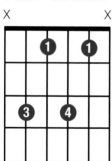

### C maj 7

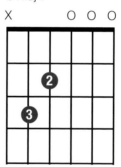

### C maj 7 b5  MOVABLE

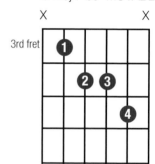

### C sus 2  MOVABLE

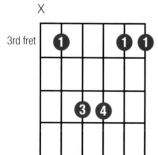

### C sus 4

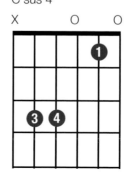

### C 7 sus 4 MOVABLE

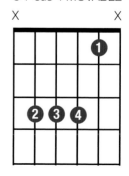

C 6  MOVABLE

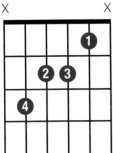

C min 6  MOVABLE

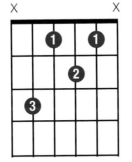

C 9 MOVABLE

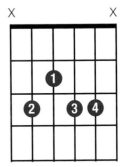

C min 9  MOVABLE

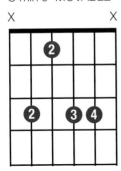

C add 9

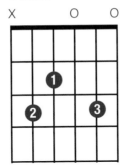

C aug  MOVABLE

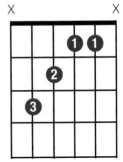

C dim  MOVABLE

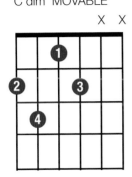

C 11  MOVABLE

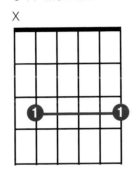

C 13  MOVABLE

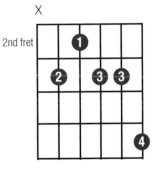

2nd fret

# D

### D maj
X X O
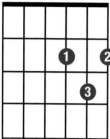

### D 7
X X O
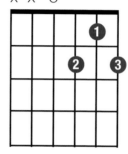

### D min
X X O
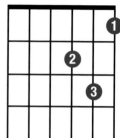

### D min 7
X X O
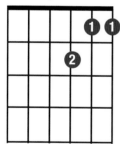

### D maj 7
X X O
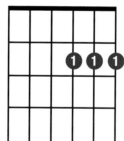

### D maj 7 b5
X X O
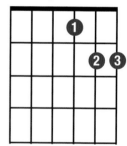

### D sus 2
X X O          O
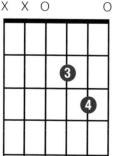

### D sus 4
X X O
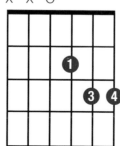

### D 7 sus 4
X X O
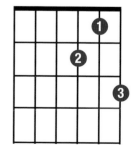

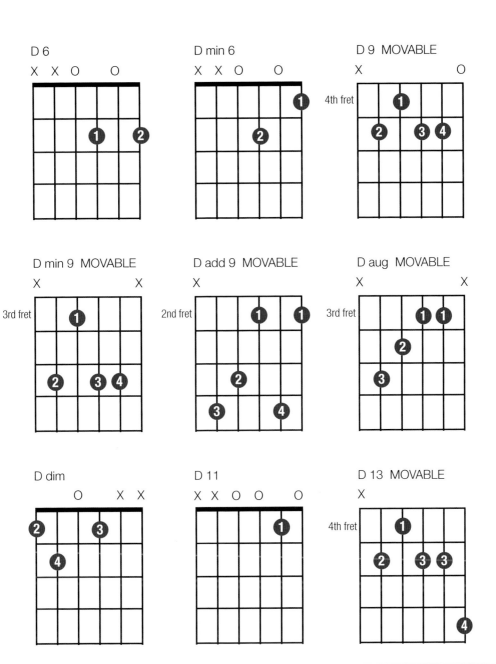

# E

### E maj

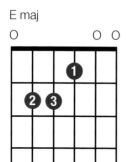

### E 7

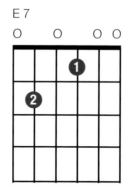

### E min

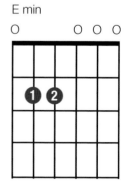

### E min 7

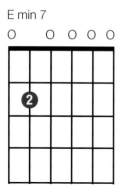

### E maj 7

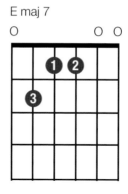

### E maj 7 b5 MOVABLE

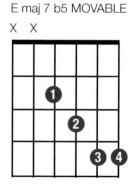

### E sus 2  MOVABLE

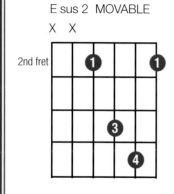

### E sus 4

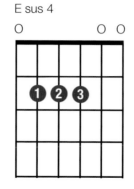

### E 7 sus 4

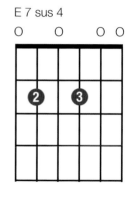

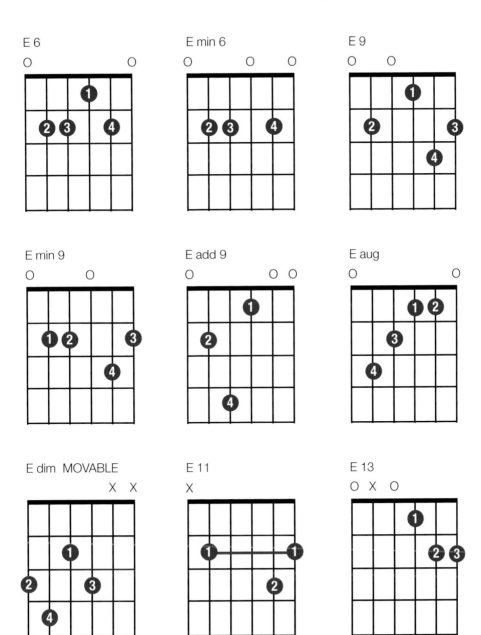

# F

### F maj MOVABLE

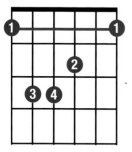

### F 7 MOVABLE

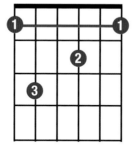

### F min MOVABLE

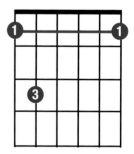

### F min 7 MOVABLE

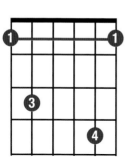

### F maj 7

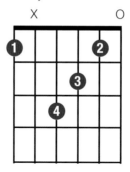

### F maj 7 b5

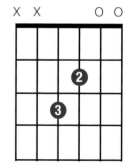

### F sus 2 MOVABLE

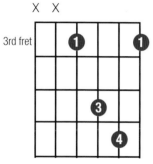

### F sus 4 MOVABLE

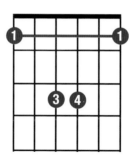

### F 7 sus 4 MOVABLE

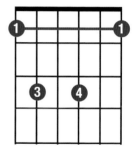

F 6  MOVABLE

X

F min 6 MOVABLE

X

E 9

O    O

F min 9  MOVABLE

F add 9  MOVABLE

F aug  MOVABLE

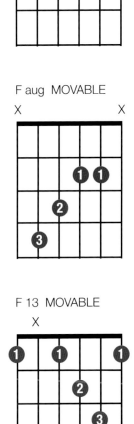

X              X

F dim

O      X  X

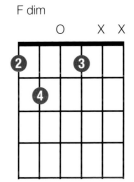

F 11  MOVABLE

X  X

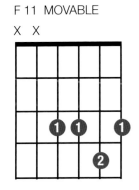

F 13  MOVABLE

X

# G

### G maj
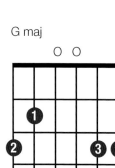

### G 7
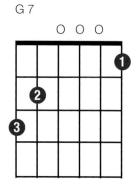

### G min  MOVABLE
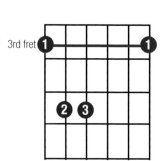

### G min 7  MOVABLE

### G maj 7  MOVABLE
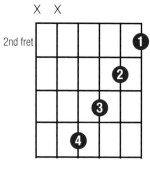

### G maj 7 b5  MOVABLE
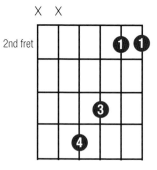

### G sus 2
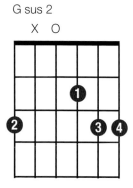

### G sus 4
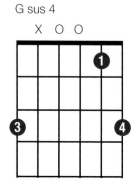

### G 7 sus 4
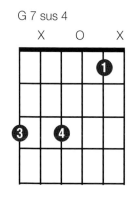

G 6

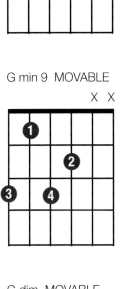

G min 6  MOVABLE

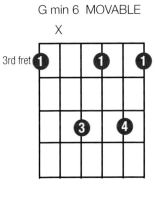

G 9  MOVABLE

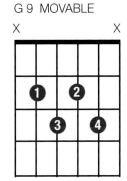

G min 9  MOVABLE

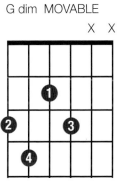

G add 9  MOVABLE

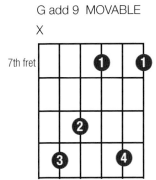

G aug

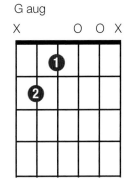

G dim  MOVABLE

G 11 MOVABLE

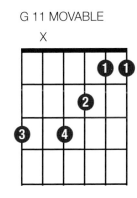

G 13

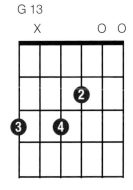

# FREQUENTLY ASKED QUESTIONS

**• When should I change my guitar strings?**

I think it's a good idea to change your strings as often as possible. Don't leave it until your strings go black and feel like barbed wire before you change them. I actually change my strings before every gig.

**• How long until I get calluses on my fingertips?**

That depends on how much you play. If you play a lot, it takes less time. In general, I believe it usually takes a few months of solid playing to harden the tips of your fingers properly. So get cracking!

**• Can a guitar ever be perfectly in tune?**

Yes. If you have a good quality guitar and it has been set up properly, you should be able to achieve a perfectly tuned guitar. On the flip side, if you want to get scientific, in tune is probably never completely attainable down to the most minute level, but to the human ear, it will sound in tune!

**• How do I play faster?**

In my opinion, playing fast is more about perfecting slow playing, then gradually increasing speed. There are a few explanations about that philosophy. Firstly, 'perfection' means perfect technique from both hands with robot-like precision. Secondly, gradually increasing speed may be done over the course of many months, not one hour. People who can play guitar at the speed of light are just the same as you, only they have trained their fingers and brain to execute their playing with great precision. It is just like learning how to walk using motor skills – you start out wobbly and end up doing it with ease, but it takes a lot of time and dedication to practice.

**• How do you write songs?**

The short answer is, any way you like!

I always relate music to cooking – if you know how to cook, you know that certain spices and ingredients complement each other. If you don't know how to cook, you may end up stumbling on an amazing creation, or make something that the snails wouldn't eat. My advice is to start listening and trying to analyse songs that you love and find out why you love them. Why does that chord work so well with that other chord? Why does that melody sound so great over that chord? To get anywhere in music, I think you have to always ask a lot of questions and try and dissect the things that appeal to you.

**• Why does my guitar always go out of tune?**

There is a lot of different ways your guitar can go out of tune. Exposing your guitar to a change in climate is probably one of the most common reasons. Every time you take it outside, you can affect the tuning. If your guitar is in a soft case and not a hard case, the bag can touch the tuning keys and put it out of tune. Obviously if you bump the tuning keys or have poor quality tuning keys that move or are loose, it can affect the tuning. If you change the gauge (thickness) of strings without having it set up for that gauge, you can put stress on the neck, which will make the guitar go out of tune.

**• Does guitar get harder from the level I am at now?**

Guitar can be as complicated as you want. You could always learn more, play more, play better. Even the greatest guitarists on earth have challenges – they just differ as you progress.

**• How long does it take to be as good as the rock stars?**

You would be surprised how many professional guitarists aren't that good! It's more about interpretation and originality in some cases, and in some cases neither. To answer your question, it all depends on which rock stars you are referring to! I would say if you learned from a good teacher and practised rigorously, you could be playing like some of today's rock stars in a couple of years.

# SUMMARY

To benefit from the Simply Guitar section, I recommend you review all the material as often as you can. Make sure you fully understand everything that has been discussed before you move on to other subjects.

The most important things to remember are the two 'Ps'; patience and practice. Be patient enough to slow things down and run them over and over, refining your technique with the tips outlined in this section and practise daily.

You will not progress if you don't practise. I cannot stress enough the importance of daily practice and a regimented, disciplined approach to doing so. Practise all of the priority topics before you mess around. Allocate a few minutes each day to focus purely on your technique. Critique your own playing – could you do that better? Is your technique as good as it could be? Does that sound as good as when your teacher plays it? 15 minutes practice Monday to Sunday is better than no practice during the week and eight hours on the weekend.

Consolidate your knowledge. I teach a lot of students things that they don't realise they already know, simply because they haven't 'joined the dots'. For example, if I can play a G major chord, I also know that the root note is a G note. Therefore, I know where the G note is on the neck. Using the musical alphabet, I can easily find F# or G# or any surrounding notes from that G note.

Make sure you think about everything you have learned and everything you know, and try and 'join the dots'. Try and apply the knowledge you have to your playing.

Listen to great guitar players. Listen to the guitar in songs that you like. Always try and define what you like about them and what you don't like. Talk to musicians. Use the internet. Buy videos and books to further your understanding of guitar. Get a good teacher. Try a few different teachers. Play with other guitar players, even if they are beginners. Teach other people what you know, because verbalising and teaching is a great way to reinforce what you yourself have learned.

Once you have understood everything that has been discussed in the Simply Guitar section, move on to the Lead Guitar section. The Lead Guitar section will help you to gain a deeper understanding of how 'improvising' and 'soloing' actually work.

# LEAD
# GUITAR

# INTRODUCTION

The aim of the Lead Guitar section is to get you improvising as quickly as possible while providing guidance towards a deeper understanding of *how* improvising actually works.

The definition of 'improvising' or 'soloing' is spontaneous musical creation – music performed without preparation. Yet every time you hear a musician 'improvise', they are playing phrases and musical concepts within a 'context' – improvisation is the spontaneous arrangement of established ideas and musical concepts.

An analogy would be speaking or communicating. When we speak, we are not saying words we have never spoken before, but we are creating sentences with words we already know in order to express ourselves. When we are young we learn how to speak, we learn words and their meanings, and then we spontaneously put all of that information together to communicate.

I have identified a common problem: guitarists often learn one scale (usually the blues scale) and then expect it to sound good when they play it over anything and everything. This is the equivalent of learning a few words and expecting them to express everything you need to say within any context.

This section is my attempt at a simple solution to this problem.

# ESSENTIAL THEORY

## GLOSSARY

The hardest part of learning anything new is familiarising yourself with, and understanding, all of the terms and expressions.

This section is designed to be your 'go to' for any terms or words you may not be familiar with. If I have failed to include something and you are scratching your head about it, try searching for it on the internet.

### *The guitar neck*

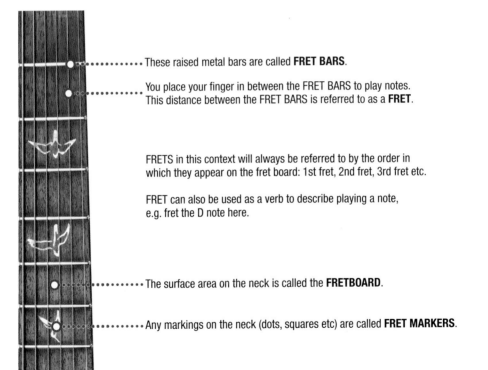

These raised metal bars are called **FRET BARS**.

You place your finger in between the FRET BARS to play notes. This distance between the FRET BARS is referred to as a **FRET**.

FRETS in this context will always be referred to by the order in which they appear on the fret board: 1st fret, 2nd fret, 3rd fret etc.

FRET can also be used as a verb to describe playing a note, e.g. fret the D note here.

The surface area on the neck is called the **FRETBOARD**.

Any markings on the neck (dots, squares etc) are called **FRET MARKERS**.

## Tab symbols

Here are the tab symbols you will come across in this book. I will provide a brief description of what each symbol means in relation to the tabbed notes in the example illustration.

### Slide down

Pick the note on the 5th fret and, while maintaining the pressure applied by your fretting finger, slide the note down to the 3rd fret without picking and without releasing any pressure by your fretting finger.

### Slide up

Pick the note on the 3rd fret and, while maintaining the pressure applied by your fretting finger, slide the note up to the 5th fret without picking and without releasing any pressure by your fretting finger.

### Hammer on

Pick the note on the 3rd fret and, while maintaining the pressure applied by your first finger, put your third finger on the 5th fret in a 'hammer' type action without picking.

### Pull off

Place your first finger on the 3rd fret and your third finger on the 5th fret. Pick the note on the 5th fret, then 'pull off' your third finger in a plucking-type action, essentially playing the note held by your first finger.

### Half step bend

Pick the note on the 3rd fret with your 3rd finger and using your first, second and third fingers bend the string upwards on the fret board until you raise the tension by a semitone.

### Whole step bend

Pick the note on the 3rd fret with your 3rd finger and using your first, second and third fingers bend the string upwards on the fret board until you raise the tension by a tone. (This can be very difficult on an acoustic guitar.)

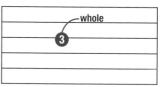

# CHORD SHAPES

Chord shapes are shown with simple diagrams indicating where to place your fingers on the fret board to form a particular chord.

**0** means play that string OPEN (with no fingers fretting any notes).

**X** means do not play that string.

The numbers tell you which fingers on your fretting hand are used.

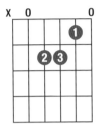

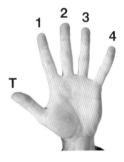

Here is the guitar neck from a frontal perspective.

Here is the chord shape above placed on the guitar neck, indicating where your fingers go.

# SCALE DIAGRAMS

Scale diagrams show the guitar neck from your playing perspective.

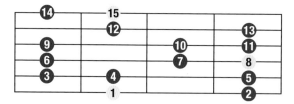

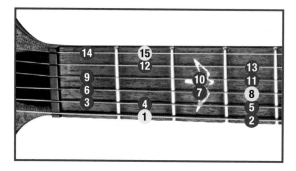

You can think of scale diagrams as an image of the guitar neck as though you had the guitar sitting flat on your lap facing upwards:

- The horizontal lines represent the strings.

- The vertical lines represent the frets.

- The circles represent where the notes of the scale appear on the fret board.

- The numbers within the circles tell you which order to play the notes.

- The light circles tell you where the 'root notes' are.

The 'root note' in a scale or a chord indicates the starting note, that is, the note that denotes which key you are in. For example, the root note of a C blues scale will be C. The root note of a D major chord will be D.

# POSITION PLAYING

Unlike chord shapes (also known as diagrams), the numbers on the diagrams on page 74 tell you in which order to play the notes, not which finger to use. To know which finger to use we implement position playing.

First position would be first finger on the 1st fret, second finger on the 2nd fret, third finger on the 3rd fret and fourth finger on the 4th fret.

Fifth position would be first finger on the 5th fret, second finger on the 6th fret, third finger on the 7th fret and fourth finger on the 8th fret.

first position

fifth position

## *How to read tablature (TAB)*

Tablature, or tab as it is commonly referred to, was around long before music notation was invented – some say it originated in China over 30,000 years ago. Tab is a very convenient way to depict how to play notes and chords on the guitar.

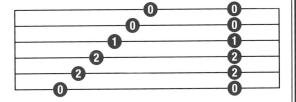

In the above diagram:

- The lines represent the strings.
- The numbers tell you which fret to play (remember, O means OPEN string).
- When the numbers are stacked on top of each other, they show a chord.

# WHAT YOU NEED TO KNOW ABOUT CHORDS

Chords are three or more notes played simultaneously. That means technically you could play three different notes at once on a piano or a guitar and you would be playing a chord – whether or not it would sound good is another story!

All chords are created from three or more notes derived from the major scale. To really understand the structure of chords, you must first understand the major scale. An analogy for this might be: you wouldn't build a house without first knowing the architectural plans.

Right now you need to know the following:

- Chords are created from three or more notes derived from the major scale. These notes are arranged into formulas or, as I like to think of them, 'recipes'.

- You can break chords up into three main groups: major, minor and dominant.

These three chord groups have their own distinct sounds, much like flavours have their own distinct tastes. To have sweet you would use sugar, to have savoury you would use salt and to have sour you would use something acidic, like vinegar.

Chords are the same: to have major chords you use the 1st, 3rd and 5th notes of the major scale (Formula = 1, 3, 5), *creating a 'happy' sound.*

To have minor chords you use the 1st, flattened 3rd and 5th notes of the major scale (Formula = 1, ♭3, 5), *creating a 'sad' sound.*

To have dominant chords you use the 1st, 3rd, 5th and flattened 7th notes of the major scale (Formula = 1, 3, 5, ♭7), *creating a 'bluesy' sound.*

You may be wondering what a flattened 3rd is. Put your finger on the 5th fret of the high E string. This note is A. Move up one fret and the note becomes A sharp (A♯), that is, you have 'sharpened' the note by moving it up one fret. Now go back to the A note (A natural). Now move back one fret. You are now playing A flat (A♭), that is, you have 'flattened' the note by moving back a fret.

| A♭ | A | A♯ |
|------|---------|-------|
| flat | natural | sharp |
| ← | | → |

| | 1 | 3 | 5 | |
|----------|---|----|---|----|
| major | 1 | 3 | 5 | |
| minor | 1 | ♭3 | 5 | |
| dominant | 1 | 3 | 5 | ♭7 |

All chords are extensions or variations of these three basic chord formulas. I will include formulas with all of the chords mentioned in this book. Even if you don't fully understand them yet, try to remember what they are.

# WHAT YOU NEED TO KNOW ABOUT SCALES

Like chords, scales are also referenced from the major scale. Here are all of the notes in Western music (the musical alphabet):

| A | A♯ | B | C | C♯ | D | D♯ | E | F | F♯ | G | G♯ |
|---|----|---|---|----|---|----|---|---|----|---|----|

After G♯ you end up back at A, only an octave higher in pitch. What is an octave? Sing the intro riff of the song 'My Sharona' by The Knack or the opening two notes of 'Somewhere over the Rainbow'. These notes are the same but one is higher in pitch – that is an octave. (There is a more theoretical explanation, but I'll get to that later – see page 81.)

To relate this to guitar, play the low E string open and then count up through the musical alphabet until you reach the 12th fret. Every note on the 12th fret is exactly one octave higher than the open strings.

Before I elaborate on this, there are a couple of terms you need to know: tones and semitones.

Tones and semitones both describe distance between one note and the next, for example, moving one tone up from A will give you B:

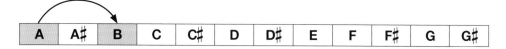

Moving one tone up from C♯ will give you D♯:

Moving one semitone up from B will give you C:

Moving one semitone up from D will give you D♯:

On guitar this is even easier:

- To move up a tone, just move up 2 frets.

- To move up a semitone, just move up 1 fret.

> The other name for a tone is a 'whole step'.
>
> The other name for a semitone is 'half step'.

Now that you know about tones (whole steps) and semitones (half steps) I can explain how scale formulas work.

The major scale is like the mother ship. Everything is derived and referenced from it. The formula for a major scale looks like this:

*Tone, Tone, Semitone, Tone, Tone, Tone, Semitone.*

I will colour the notes that fall on the formula starting from A using the musical alphabet:

In this case, the scale would be A major because the formula was started on an A note.

Relating this back to guitar, starting from the open A string and moving up, the Tone, Tone, Semitone, Tone, Tone, Tone, Semitone formula would look like this:

## A little more on chords

Here are the notes of the A major scale:

| A | B | C# | D | E | F# | G# | A |
|---|---|----|---|---|----|----|----|
| 1 | 2 | 3  | 4 | 5 | 6  | 7  | 8 |

I have numbered each note to show you how chord formulas relate to the major scale.

The notes in an A major chord would be: A, C#, E (1, 3, 5):

| A | B | C# | D | E | F# | G# | A |
|---|---|----|---|---|----|----|----|
| 1 | 2 | 3  | 4 | 5 | 6  | 7  | 8 |

The notes in an A minor chord would be: A, C, E (1, ♭3, 5):

| A | B | C  | D | E | F# | G# | A |
|---|---|----|---|---|----|----|----|
| 1 | 2 | ♭3 | 4 | 5 | 6  | 7  | 8 |

Notice how the C# becomes a C because of the ♭3rd (flattened 3rd).

## More on octaves

Earlier I suggested you sing the opening line from 'My Sharona' or 'Somewhere over the Rainbow' to hear an octave. Now I can explain what an octave is in more detail.

Oct = 8, for example, an octopus has eight tentacles and an octagon has eight sides. An octave, then, is the 8th note of a major scale played against or simultaneously with the 1st note of the major scale.

A common abbreviation of the major scale formula is: T, T, S, T, T, T, S (T = Tone, S = Semitone).

Let's start the formula on a D note in the musical alphabet:

| D | D# | E | F | F# | G | G# | A | A# | B | C | C# | D |
|---|----|---|---|----|---|----|---|----|---|---|----|---|

    T      T    S    T    T    T    S

In this case, the scale would be D major because the formula was started on a D note.

These past few pages have had a lot of information to take in, but these are important topics to cover in order to understand the explanations of the fun stuff we are heading towards.

**Note:** When abbreviated, 'minor' is always written with a lower case 'm'. major is always written with an upper case 'M'.

# BASIC ROCK IMPROVISATION

## THE 12 BAR BLUES IN THE KEY OF A – VERSION 1

The 12 Bar Blues is a chord progression, 12 bars in length.

A chord progression is a series of chords that sound good together and 'progress' towards a sound of 'resolution'.

A 'bar' refers to music notation. One bar of music usually contains 4 beats, for example, '1, 2, 3, 4'.

I am going to show you two versions of the 12 Bar Blues, both in the key of A. Version 1 has a very simple harmony (only two notes at a time). Version 2 has chords (three or more notes at a time) – we will look at this later in the 'More Complex Improvisation' section.

Here is version 1:

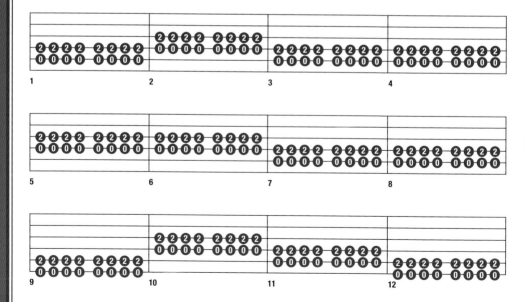

# TWO SHAPES OF THE
# A BLUES SCALE

The blues scale is very similar to another scale called the minor pentatonic scale. Pentatonic scales contain just 5 notes (pentagram = 5 points, pentagon = 5 sides).

Blues scales are identical to minor pentatonic scales except for the addition of a flattened 5th note (the blues note), making the blues scale a 6 note scale.

There are five shapes of the pentatonic and blues scales. These shapes are also referred to as 'patterns'. Every shape contains exactly the same notes; they just appear in different places depending on what position you are playing in.

We are going to learn two of the most commonly used blues scale shapes.

## Shape 1

Play the first scale shape starting on the 5th fret.

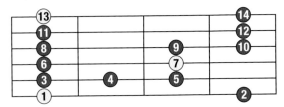

## Shape 2

The second shape starts on the 2nd note of the first scale shape (starting on the 8th fret).

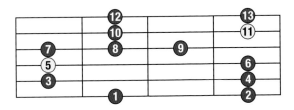

These two scale shapes are 'moveable' shapes that can be played anywhere on the neck. I have coloured the root notes lighter to help you identify where you would move them relative to the key you are playing in.

# START IMPROVISING!

Record yourself slowly playing the 12 Bar Blues in the key of A.

Practise playing the two blues scale shapes (as written on page 85) over the top of the recorded 12 Bar Blues in A.

Practise playing this scale forwards and backwards in a constant and consistent rhythm over the 12 Bar Blues.

When you start to feel confident with the scale, start exploring what you can do with it creatively. Notice what sounds good and what sounds bad. Explore and exhaust your options as this scale is going to be your friend for a long time!

**Tip:** Try incorporating hammer ons, pull offs, bends and slides into your improvisation to add more expression.

# WHAT ARE LICKS?

In improvisation, a lick is similar to a quote or saying in speech, that is, an established concept that you apply to relevant circumstances when they arise.

Think about the main guitar riff in the song 'Johnny B Good'. This riff is a short melodic idea that is dynamic, has impact and can be reused over and over. This is referred to as a 'lick'.

This and the following entry include a selection of 18 popular licks to memorise that are useable over the 12 Bar Blues. Each lick is derived from the two blues scale shapes you have already learnt. (Note: You may encounter a note here and there that is not directly found in the 6 note blues scale.)

Try to be creative with mixing and matching them together.

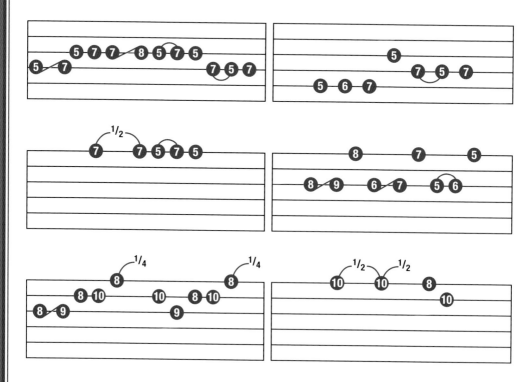

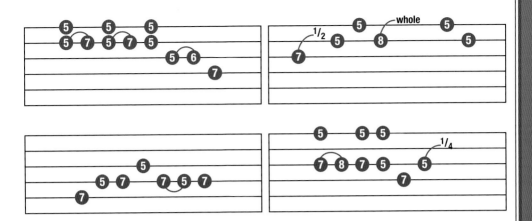

## MORE LICKS

All of these licks are moveable (that is, they can be played in other keys), but for the purposes of this book I have written them in the key of A.

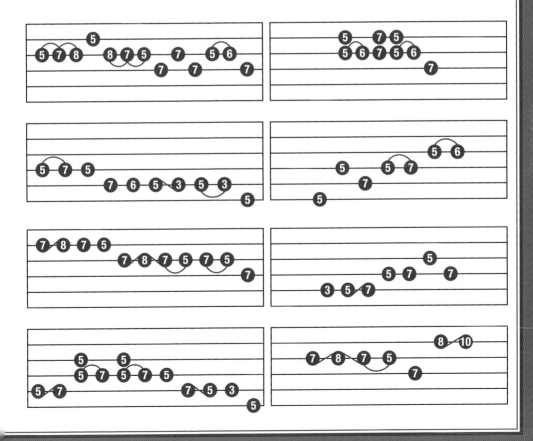

# More Complex Improvisation

## MORE ON CHORD STRUCTURE

The great thing about improvising over version 1 of the 12 Bar Blues is that you can get away with playing just the blues scale patterns and a few licks over the whole progression and sound pretty good!

This is possible because of the simple harmony of the 'power chords' you are improvising over.

A power chord is another name for a 5th interval being played in a chord-like fashion.

A 5th interval is simply the 1st and the 5th notes of the major scale. Refer to page 77 and see the chord formulas for major, minor and dominant 7th. The consistent ingredients in these chords are the 1 and the 5. This interval is called a 5th or a 'perfect 5th' because the sound is so resolved and complete. Think of the opening two notes from the *Star Wars* theme; this is an example of a 5th interval – very powerful!

As discussed previously, a basic chord is made up of three notes. This basic chord is called a triad (tri = 3 – think tripod, trimester, triangle etc).

Here are the major and minor triad formulas that we learnt on page 77:

| major | 1 | 3 | 5 |
|-------|---|------|---|
| minor | 1 | ♭3 | 5 |

Notice that the difference between a major and a minor chord is dependent on whether the 3rd is natural or flattened. A natural 3rd will make the chord sound happy while a flattened 3rd will make the chord sound sad.

> The word 'harmony' derives from a Greek word roughly meaning 'in agreement' or 'in balance'. In music, harmony relates to two or more notes being played simultaneously or against each other.

Next we have the most common 7th chord formulas:

| major 7 | 1 | 3 | 5 | 7 |
|---|---|---|---|---|
| dominant 7 | 1 | 3 | 5 | ♭7 |
| minor 7 | 1 | ♭3 | 5 | ♭7 |

We now know that the difference between a major and minor chord is whether the 3rd is flattened or not, and that this affects the overall sound or mood of the chord. Observe the difference between a major7 chord and a dominant 7th chord. The 7th is flattened in a dominant 7th chord.

The sound difference between a major7 and a dominant7 is also quite substantial. The major 7th chord sound is used in a lot of lounge music. Think of the first chord in 'Girl from Ipanema' – it's very smooth sounding. The dominant 7th chord has a more funky sound and is used extensively across all popular genres of music.

*In summary:*

The 1st tells you what the root of the chord is.
The 3rd determines whether the chord is happy or sad.
The 5th adds foundation to the 1st.
The 7th determines whether the chord is smooth sounding or funky.

To fully understand all of this I always imagine a house:
The 1st is the location of the house.
The 3rd is who lives there – a happy person or a sad person.
The 5th is the bricks and mortar.
The 7th is how the house is decorated – retro smooth or funky shagpile!

*Extensions*

Next we have the most common 'extensions' for major chords. Extensions are the notes that are added after a 7th (they always appear in this order = 9, 11, 13).

To avoid confusion, I'll show you how the numbering of extensions works. I will use the C major scale as an example.

| C | D | E | F | G | A | B | C |
|---|---|---|---|---|---|---|---|
| 1 | 2 | 3 | 4 | 5 | 6 | 7 | 8/1 |

You can see that C is the first note, D is the second note, E is the third note and so on.

Extensions are made from the notes of the major scale only up the second octave and numbered sequentially.

| C | D | E | F | G | A | B | C | D | E | F | G | A | B | C |
|---|---|---|---|---|---|---|---|---|---|---|---|---|---|---|
| 1 | 2 | 3 | 4 | 5 | 6 | 7 | 8/1 | 9/2 | 10/3 | 11/4 | 12/5 | 13/6 | 14/7 | 15/1 |

You will notice how the 9th is the same note as the 2nd, the 11th is the same as the 4th and the 13th is the same as the 6th.

| C | D | E | F | G | A | B | C | D | E | F | G | A | B | C |
|---|---|---|---|---|---|---|---|---|---|---|---|---|---|---|
| 1 | 2 | 3 | 4 | 5 | 6 | 7 | 8/1 | 9/2 | 10/3 | 11/4 | 12/5 | 13/6 | 14/7 | 15/1 |

The 2, 4 and 6 might be the same notes as the 9, 11 and 13, but they are an octave lower in pitch and very close to the notes used in a triad (1, 3, 5). The pitch of a note is very important to how it affects the sound of a chord.

| C | D | E | F | G | A | B | C | D | E | F | G | A | B | C |
|---|---|---|---|---|---|---|---|---|---|---|---|---|---|---|
| 1 | 2 | 3 | 4 | 5 | 6 | 7 | 8/1 | 9/2 | 10/3 | 11/4 | 12/5 | 13/6 | 14/7 | 15/1 |

Imagine a crowded room full of people talking. There are a lot of people talking at the pitches of 1, 3, 5 and 7. Now imagine one person speaking at the pitch of a 2. They will be drowned out by those talking at 1 and 3 because these pitches are so close to each other. Now if the 2 was an octave higher (i.e. a 9), their voice would cut through a lot more easily because there is nothing blocking that frequency.

| | | | | | extensions | | |
|---|---|---|---|---|---|---|---|
| **major 9th** | 1 | 3 | 5 | 7 | 9 | | |
| **major 11th** | 1 | 3 | 5 | 7 | 9 | 11 | |
| **major 13th** | 1 | 3 | 5 | 7 | 9 | 11 | 13 |

Here are the most common extensions for dominant chords:

| | | | | | extensions | | |
|---|---|---|---|---|---|---|---|
| **dominant 9th** | 1 | 3 | 5 | ♭7 | 9 | | |
| **dominant 11th** | 1 | 3 | 5 | ♭7 | 9 | 11 | |
| **dominant 13th** | 1 | 3 | 5 | ♭7 | 9 | 11 | 13 |

The most common extensions for minor chords:

| | | | | | extensions | | |
|---|---|---|---|---|---|---|---|
| **minor 9th** | 1 | ♭3 | 5 | ♭7 | 9 | | |
| **minor 11th** | 1 | ♭3 | 5 | ♭7 | 9 | 11 | |
| **minor 13th** | 1 | ♭3 | 5 | ♭7 | 9 | 11 | 13 |

Observe how the only changes to the structure of these chords lies on either the 3rd or the 7th.

Also notice how in all minor chords, the 3rd and 7th notes are flattened. The only time the 7th is not flattened is when it is specifically a major7 chord.

You might be thinking a minor13 or a major13 chord has seven notes in it, yet you have only four fingers and there are only six strings!

This is where thinking of a chord as a house comes in handy. In any 13th chord (major, dominant or minor) you can generally omit the following:

- The 5th – the foundation is already being covered by the 1st.
- The 9th and 11th – the 13th is the one we want to hear.

We always need to keep:

- The 1st – this tells us where the house is.
- The 3rd – this tells us whether who lives in the house is happy or sad.
- The 7th – this tells us the vibe of the house.
- The 13th – this is the added feature to enhance the vibe of the house.

This same rule applies with the 9th and 11th – these notes are just additional features to enhance the vibe of the house.

All chords can be substituted by other chords within the same family. Here are a few examples:

**Major family**

Major chords can be substituted with major7th chords.

Major7th chords can be substituted with major9th chords.

Major9th chords can be substituted with major11th chords.

Major11th chords can be substituted with major13th chords.

(or any combination of)

**Dominant 7th family**

7th chords can be substituted for 9th chords.

9th chords can be substituted for 11th chords.

11th chords can be substituted for 13th chords.

(or any combination of)

**Minor family**

minor chords can be substituted with minor7th chords.

minor7th chords can be substituted with minor9th chords.

minor9th chords can be substituted with minor11th chords.

minor11th chords can be substituted with minor13th chords.

(or any combination of)

# THE 12 BAR BLUES IN THE KEY OF A – VERSION 2 (CHORDS)

These chord shapes can be played anywhere on the neck.
The first note (root) will give the chord its name.

### Dom7 Chord (dominant 7th)

Root note on the E string

**Formula: 1, 3, 5, ♭7**

### 9 Chord (dominant 9th)

Root note on the A string

**Formula: 1, 3, 5, ♭7, 9**

The following diagrams show *where* to play each of these chords in order to play the 12 Bar Blues in A:

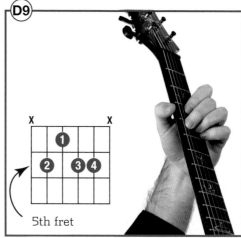

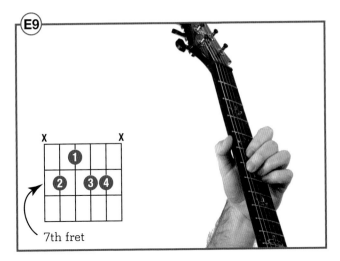

E9

X          X

① 
② ③④

7th fret

Here is the order in which you play these chords for the
12 Bar Blues:

| A7 | D9 | A7 | A7 |
|----|----|----|----|
| 1  | 2  | 3  | 4  |

| D9 | D9 | A7 | A7 |
|----|----|----|----|
| 5  | 6  | 7  | 8  |

| E9 | D9 | A7 | E9 |
|----|----|----|----|
| 9  | 10 | 11 | 12 |

Each block represents a bar of music, which has four counts. In
other words, you strum each chord four times within the bar.

| A7 | D9 | A7 | A7 |
|------|------|------|------|
| //// | //// | //// | //// |

| D9 | D9 | A7 | A7 |
|------|------|------|------|
| //// | //// | //// | //// |

| E9 | D9 | A7 | E9 |
|------|------|------|------|
| //// | //// | //// | //// |

When you become used to playing the 12 Bar Blues chord
progression, you will start to recognise many songs that use
this chord progression, especially rock and roll from the
1950s onwards (from Elvis to ACDC).

If you find the moveable chord shapes too difficult, here are some non-moveable simple shapes, which are easier ways to play the chords needed for the A 12 Bar Blues:

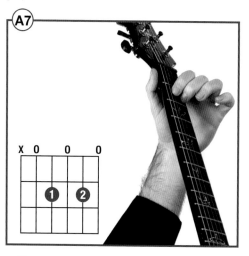

Notice that instead of D9 and E9, I have written D7 and E7.

D9 can be substituted for D7 and vice versa. An extended version of a 7th chord is a 9th chord and the two can be substituted for each other.

7th chord formula: 1, 3, 5, ♭7
9th chord formula: 1, 3, 5, ♭7, 9

# NUTS AND BOLTS OF IMPROVISATION

In this book I am only going to explore the 12 Bar Blues in the key of A, but my aim is to provide you with the tools to take things a lot further on your own. By understanding the mechanics of improvising over chords, you won't be limited by anything you have rote learnt.

Unlike the power chords or 5th chords used in version 1 of the 12 Bar Blues, version 2 of the 12 Bar Blues has chords with more complex harmony. The notes that make up the chords require special attention when you are improvising over them. If you have wondered why sometimes the blues scale works over songs and sometimes it doesn't . . . here's why!

Let's break apart each chord and compare it to the A blues scale we used earlier. The A blues scale has these notes:

| A | A♯ | B | C | C♯ | D | D♯ | E | F | F♯ | G | G♯ |
|---|----|---|---|----|---|----|---|---|----|---|----|
| 1 |    |   | ♭3 |   | 4 | ♭5 | 5 |   |    | ♭7 |    |

An 'A7' chord has these notes:

| A | A♯ | B | C | C♯ | D | D♯ | E | F | F♯ | G | G♯ |
|---|----|---|---|----|---|----|---|---|----|---|----|
| 1 |    |   |   | 3 |   |    | 5 |   |    | ♭7 |    |

The notes I have coloured *green* in the A blues scale will clash with the notes in the A7 chord:

| A | A♯ | B | C | C♯ | D | D♯ | E | F | F♯ | G | G♯ |
|---|----|---|---|----|---|----|---|---|----|---|----|
| 1 |    |   | ♭3 |   | 4 | ♭5 | 5 |   |    | ♭7 |    |

The C note in the blues scale will clash with the C♯ note in the A7 chord because it is the 3rd of the chord, and as we have learnt, the 3rd is a *very* important ingredient in defining the sound of any chord.

The A7 has a happy-sounding 3rd and the blues scale has a sad ♭3rd. This conflict creates an 'off' sounding note in the scale akin to when a singer sings a bung note.

> The D♯ note I have coloured yellow is considered the 'blues note' or 'blue note', which technically clashes a lot of the time anyway – its purpose is to create tension, which can sound really cool. Treat this note like a hot coal – you don't hold it too long!

Here is the same comparison with the A blues scale and the D7 chord.

A blues scale:

| A | A♯ | B | C | C♯ | D | D♯ | E | F | F♯ | G | G♯ |
|---|---|---|---|---|---|---|---|---|---|---|---|
| 1 |   |   | ♭3 |   | 4 | ♭5 | 5 |   |   | ♭7 |   |

D7 chord:

| D | D♯ | E | F | F♯ | G | G♯ | A | A♯ | B | C | C♯ |
|---|---|---|---|---|---|---|---|---|---|---|---|
| 1 |   |   |   | 3 |   |   | 5 |   |   | ♭7 |   |

The A blues scale does not contain the 3rd of the D7 chord. This isn't so much a clash as it is an important ingredient missing.

Here is the same comparison with the A blues scale and the E7 chord.

A blues scale:

| A | A♯ | B | C | C♯ | D | D♯ | E | F | F♯ | G | G♯ |
|---|---|---|---|---|---|---|---|---|---|---|---|
| 1 |   |   | ♭3 |   | 4 | ♭5 | 5 |   |   | ♭7 |   |

E7 chord:

| E | F | F♯ | G | G♯ | A | A♯ | B | C | C♯ | D | D♯ |
|---|---|---|---|---|---|---|---|---|---|---|---|
| 1 |   |   |   | 3 |   |   | 5 |   |   | ♭7 |   |

This time there is a G note in the A blues scale and the 3rd note of the E7 chord is a G♯. When one 3rd and another 3rd clash, it's like a personality clash and that always ends up being no good!

Now I have pointed out the problems, it's time for some solutions!

# WHAT SCALE OVER WHICH CHORD?

The previous pages of this book have all been leading to this point. The information you are about to read will help you understand the mechanics of scales and their relationship to chords in a way that should allow you to explore improvisation on your own.

We have established that the A blues scale will not work perfectly over all of the chords in the A 12 Bar Blues. Unfortunately, there is no magical scale at all that will work perfectly over any chord progression.

Here is one way I approach this dilemma. I've broken it down into seven steps:

1. Establish what key you are playing in: e.g. an A blues is in the key of A.

2. Write down the major scale notes of that key: e.g. A major.

3. Write down the major scale in two octaves that the chord you are improvising over is derived from: e.g. if playing over A7, write out the A major scale in two octaves. If playing over E7, write out the E major scale in two octaves.

4. Map out the notes of the chord you are improvising over in its full-extended form: e.g. E7 chord notes plus extensions – 1, 3, 5, b7, 9, 11, 13.

5. Compare the notes of the major scale of the key you are playing in (e.g. A major) with the notes from the chord you are improvising over (e.g. E7 and its extensions).

6. Arrange the notes of the chord you are improvising over in the same order as the major scale notes of the key you playing in (alphabetically).

7. Reconstruct the major scale of the key adding in the notes from the chord you are improvising over.

On the following pages we will go through this seven-step process with each chord in the A 12 Bar Blues.

If you want to bypass the theory of *why* things are the way they are and just get on with learning scales that work over the chords in the A 12 Bar Blues, then go straight to the Cheat Sheet section on page 114.

# WHAT SCALE OVER A7?

**Step 1:** *Establish what key you are playing in.*

A, because we are playing an A 12 Bar Blues.

**Step 2:** *Write down the major scale notes of that key.*

To find the notes in the A major scale, write out the musical alphabet starting from A and colour the notes according to the formula for a major scale that we learnt about on page 80:

Tone, Tone, Semitone, Tone, Tone, Tone, Semitone

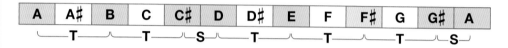

The notes of the A major scale are:

| A | B | C♯ | D | E | F♯ | G♯ | A |
|---|---|----|---|---|----|----|---|
| 1 | 2 | 3  | 4 | 5 | 6  | 7  | 8 |

**Step 3:** *Write down the major scale in two octaves that the chord you are playing over is derived from.*

The A7 chord formula is derived from the A major scale so the notes are:

| A | B | C♯ | D | E | F♯ | G | A | B | C♯ | D | E | F♯ | G |
|---|---|----|---|---|----|---|---|---|----|---|---|----|---|
| 1 | 2 | 3 | 4 | 5 | 6 | 7 | 8 | 9 | 10 | 11 | 12 | 13 | 14 |

A major scale

**Step 4:** *Map out the notes of the chord you are playing over in its full-extended form.*

The formula for a 7th chord is:

| 1 | 3 | 5 | ♭7 |
|---|---|---|---|

Extending a 7th chord out will give us:

| 1 | 3 | 5 | ♭7 | 9 | 11 | 13 |
|---|---|---|---|---|---|---|

Therefore the notes are going to be:

| A | B | C♯ | D | E | F♯ | G | A | B | C♯ | D | E | F♯ | G |
|---|---|----|---|---|----|---|---|---|----|---|---|----|---|
| 1 | 2 | 3 | 4 | 5 | 6 | ♭7 | 8 | 9 | 10 | 11 | 12 | 13 | 14 |

Notice I changed the 7th note of the A major scale which is a G♯, to a G to make it a ♭7 according to the formula of a 7th chord.

All of the notes belonging to A7 are:

| A | C♯ | E | G | B | D | F♯ |
|---|----|---|---|---|---|----|

**Step 5:** *Compare the notes of the A major scale with the notes from the A7 chord.*

The highlighted boxes show all of the chord extensions.

| A major scale | A | B | C♯ | D | E | F♯ | G♯ | A |
|---------------|---|---|----|---|---|----|----|---|
| interval | 1 | 2 | 3 | 4 | 5 | 6 | 7 | 8 |

| A7 chord | A | C♯ | E | G | B | D | F♯ |
|----------|---|----|---|---|---|---|----|
| A7 formula | 1 | 3 | 5 | ♭7 | 9 | 11 | 13 |

**Step 6:** *Arrange the notes of the A7 chord in the same order as the A major scale (alphabetically).*

| A7 chord | A | B | C♯ | D | E | F♯ | G |
|---|---|---|---|---|---|---|---|
| A7 formula | 1 | 9 | 5 | 11 | 5 | 13 | ♭7 |

**Step 7:** *Reconstruct the A major scale adding in the notes from the A7 chord.*

| reconstructed major scale | A | B | C♯ | D | E | F♯ | G | A |
|---|---|---|---|---|---|---|---|---|
| reconstructed major scale formula | 1 | 2 | 3 | 4 | 5 | 6 | ♭7 | 8 |

I've highlighted the only difference between the A7 chord notes and the A major scale.

The scale to play over A7 is an A major scale with a ♭7.

| formula | 1 | 2 | 3 | 4 | 5 | 6 | ♭7 | 8 |
|---|---|---|---|---|---|---|---|---|

This formula gives us something called the Mixolydian mode. On page 111 we will learn what modes are and how they work. In the meantime, it is okay for you to know that a major scale with a ♭7 is called a Mixolydian mode.

Therefore, over A7 in the A 12 Bar Blues, you would use an A Mixolydian scale to improvise.

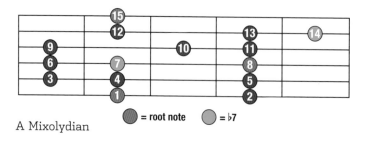

A Mixolydian

# WHAT SCALE OVER D7?

**Step 1:** *Establish what key you are playing in.*

We are playing an A 12 Bar Blues.

**Step 2:** *Write down the major scale notes of that key.*

The notes of the A major scale are:

| A | B | C♯ | D | E | F♯ | G♯ | A |
|---|---|----|---|---|----|----|---|
| 1 | 2 | 3  | 4 | 5 | 6  | 7  | 8 |

**Step 3:** *Write down the major scale in two octaves that the chord you are playing over is derived from.*

The D7 chord formula is derived from the D major scale so the notes are:

| D | D♯ | E | F | F♯ | G | G♯ | A | A♯ | B | C | C♯ | D |
|---|----|---|---|----|---|----|---|----|---|---|----|---|
| T | | T | | S | | T | | T | | T | | S |

| D | E | F♯ | G | A | B | C♯ | D |
|---|---|----|---|---|---|----|---|
| 1 | 2 | 3  | 4 | 5 | 6 | 7  | 8 |

D major scale

**Step 4:** *Map out the notes of the chord you are playing over in its full-extended form.*

The formula for a 7th chord is:

| 1 | 3 | 5 | ♭7 |
|---|---|---|---|

Extending a 7th chord out will give us:

| 1 | 3 | 5 | ♭7 | 9 | 11 | 13 |
|---|---|---|----|---|----|----|

To find the notes of a D7 chord fully extended, we need to map out the D major scale in two octaves then highlight the chord formula:

| D | E | F♯ | G | A | B | C | D | E | F♯ | G | A | B | C♯ |
|---|---|----|---|---|---|---|---|---|----|---|---|---|----|
| 1 | 2 | 3  | 4 | 5 | 6 | ♭7| 8 | 9 | 10 | 11| 12| 13| 14 |

Notice I changed the 7th note of the D major scale which is a C♯ (see Figure 2), to a C to make it a ♭7 according to the formula of a 7th chord.

All of the notes belonging to D7 are:

| D | F♯ | A | C | E | G | B |
|---|----|---|---|---|---|---|

**Step 5:** *Compare the notes of the A major scale with the notes from the D7 chord.*

The highlighted boxes show all of the chord's extensions.

| A major scale | A | B | C♯ | D | E | F♯ | G♯ | A |
|---------------|---|---|----|---|---|----|----|---|
| interval      | 1 | 2 | 3  | 4 | 5 | 6  | 7  | 8 |

| D7 chord   | D | F♯ | A | C  | E | G  | B  |
|------------|---|----|---|----|---|----|----|
| D7 formula | 1 | 3  | 5 | ♭7 | 9 | 11 | 13 |

**Step 6:** *Arrange the notes of the D7 chord in the same order as the A major scale notes (alphabetically).*

| D7 chord | A | B | C | D | E | F♯ | G |
|---|---|---|---|---|---|---|---|
| D7 formula | 5 | 13 | ♭7 | 1 | 9 | 3 | 11 |

**Step 7:** *Reconstruct the A major scale adding in the notes from the D7 chord.*

| reconstructed major scale | A | B | C | D | E | F♯ | G | A |
|---|---|---|---|---|---|---|---|---|
| reconstructed major scale formula | 1 | 2 | ♭3 | 4 | 5 | 6 | ♭7 | 8 |

I've highlighted the only difference between the D7 chord notes and the A major scale.

The scale to play over D7 is an A major scale with a ♭3 and ♭7.

| formula | 1 | 2 | ♭3 | 4 | 5 | 6 | ♭7 | 8 |
|---|---|---|---|---|---|---|---|---|

This formula gives us the Dorian mode. Therefore, over D7 in the A 12 Bar Blues you would use an A Dorian mode to improvise.

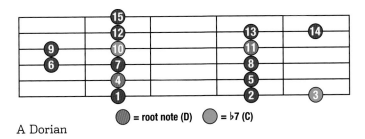

A Dorian

# WHAT SCALE OVER E7?

**Step 1:** *Establish what key you are playing in.*

A.

**Step 2:** *Write down the major scale notes of that key.*

The notes of the A major scale are:

| A | B | C♯ | D | E | F♯ | G♯ | A |
|---|---|----|---|---|----|----|---|
| 1 | 2 | 3  | 4 | 5 | 6  | 7  | 8 |

**Step 3:** *Write down the major scale in two octaves that the chord you are playing over is derived from.*

The E7 chord formula is derived from the E major scale so the notes are:

| E | F | F♯ | G | G♯ | A | A♯ | B | C | C♯ | D | D♯ | E |
|---|---|----|---|----|---|----|---|---|----|---|----|---|
| T | | T | | S | | T | | T | | T | | S |

| E | F♯ | G♯ | A | B | C♯ | D♯ | E |
|---|----|----|---|---|----|----|---|
| 1 | 2  | 3  | 4 | 5 | 6  | 7  | 8 |

E major scale

**Step 4:** *Map out the notes of the chord you are playing over in its full-extended form.*

The formula for a 7th chord is:

| 1 | 3 | 5 | ♭7 |
|---|---|---|---|

Extending a 7th chord out will give us:

| 1 | 3 | 5 | ♭7 | 9 | 11 | 13 |
|---|---|---|----|---|----|----|

To find the notes of an E7 chord fully extended, we need to map out the E major scale in two octaves, then highlight the chord formula:

| E | F♯ | G♯ | A | B | C♯ | D | E | F♯ | G♯ | A | B | C♯ | D♯ |
|---|----|----|---|---|----|---|---|----|----|---|---|----|----|
| 1 | 2  | 3  | 4 | 5 | 6  | ♭7 | 8 | 9  | 10 | 11 | 12 | 13 | 14 |

Notice I changed the 7th note of the E major scale, which is a D♯ (see Figure 3), to a D to make it a ♭7 according to the formula of a 7th chord.

All of the notes belonging to E7 are:

| E | G♯ | B | D | F♯ | A | C♯ |
|---|----|---|---|----|---|----|

**Step 5:** *Compare the notes of the A major scale with the notes from the E7 chord.*

The highlighted boxes show all of the chord's extensions.

| A major scale | A | B | C♯ | D | E | F♯ | G♯ | A |
|---------------|---|---|----|---|---|----|----|---|
| interval      | 1 | 2 | 3  | 4 | 5 | 6  | 7  | 8 |

| E7 chord   | E | G♯ | B | D  | F♯ | A  | C♯ |
|------------|---|----|---|----|----|----|----|
| E7 formula | 1 | 3  | 5 | ♭7 | 9  | 11 | 13 |

**Step 6:** *Arrange the notes of the E7 chord in the same order as the A major scale notes (alphabetically).*

| E7 chord | A | B | C♯ | D | E | F♯ | G♯ |
|---|---|---|---|---|---|---|---|
| E7 formula | 11 | 5 | 13 | ♭7 | 1 | 9 | 3 |

**Step 7:** *Reconstruct the A major scale adding in the notes from the E7 chord.*

| reconstructed major scale | A | B | C♯ | D | E | F♯ | G♯ | A |
|---|---|---|---|---|---|---|---|---|
| reconstructed major scale formula | 1 | 2 | 3 | 4 | 5 | 6 | 7 | 8 |

The E7 chord notes are identical to the notes of the A major scale.

The scale to play over E7 is an A major scale.

| **formula** | 1 | 2 | 3 | 4 | 5 | 6 | 7 | 8 |
|---|---|---|---|---|---|---|---|---|

The major scale is also known as the Ionian mode. Therefore, over E7 in the A 12 Bar Blues you would use an A Ionian mode to improvise.

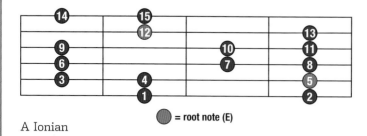

A Ionian

⬤ = root note (E)

# WHAT ARE MODES?

People have written books on modes alone, so I will try to keep this explanation brief.

Modes are scales derived from the notes of the major scale. There are seven modes because a major scale has seven notes. Each mode plays through the major scale notes, only starting and finishing on a different degree. For example, here are the notes in the C major scale:

| C | D | E | F | G | A | B |
|---|---|---|---|---|---|---|
| 1 | 2 | 3 | 4 | 5 | 6 | 7 |

If I map out the notes of the C major scale starting on each degree, I will get the seven major modes:

| Ionian | C | D | E | F | G | A | B |
|---|---|---|---|---|---|---|---|
| Dorian | D | E | F | G | A | B | C |
| Phrygian | E | F | G | A | B | C | D |
| Lydian | F | G | A | B | C | D | E |
| Mixolydian | G | A | B | C | D | E | F |
| Aeolian | A | B | C | D | E | F | G |
| Locrian | B | C | D | E | F | G | A |

Here's the same thing, but I have coloured each note to make the pattern clearer:

| | | | | | | | |
|------------|---|---|---|---|---|---|---|
| Ionian | C | D | E | F | G | A | B |
| Dorian | D | E | F | G | A | B | C |
| Phrygian | E | F | G | A | B | C | D |
| Lydian | F | G | A | B | C | D | E |
| Mixolydian | G | A | B | C | D | E | F |
| Aeolian | A | B | C | D | E | F | G |
| Locrian | B | C | D | E | F | G | A |

So you can see:

| | |
|---|------------|
| C | Ionian |
| D | Dorian |
| E | Phrygian |
| F | Lydian |
| G | Mixolydian |
| A | Aeolian |
| B | Locrian |

The more you hear modes, the more you hear moods, much as minor chords sound sad and major chords sound happy. For example:

| mode name | Ionian |
|-------------|--------------------------------------------------------------------------------------------------------------------|
| formula | 1, 2, 3, 4, 5, 6, 7 |
| description | Sounds happy because it is exactly the same as the major scale. It also contains the notes needed to make all major chords. |

| mode name | Dorian |
|-------------|--------------------------------------------------------------------------------------------------------------------|
| formula | 1, 2, ♭3, 4, 5, 6, ♭7 |
| description | To me, this sounds like a more sophisticated version of the pentatonic scale. Before I knew what Dorian was, I found I was already playing it. This mode articulates the sound of a minor 7th chord because it shares the same notes (1, ♭3, 5, ♭7). |

| mode name | Phrygian |
|---|---|
| formula | 1, ♭2, ♭3, 4, 5, ♭6, ♭7 |
| description | Has a very Spanish sound to it. Like the kind of mode Zorro would play if he was improvising! This is because of the tension created by the ♭2 and ♭6. |

| mode name | Lydian |
|---|---|
| formula | 1, 2, 3, ♯4, 5, 6, 7 |
| description | This sounds mystical to me, with a sort of 'wondrous' sound. This mode is closely related to the major scale because it is virtually identical, but with a sharpened 4th. |

| mode name | Mixolydian |
|---|---|
| formula | 1, 2, 3, 4, 5, 6, ♭7 |
| description | Goes hand in hand with a dominant 7th chord because it shares the same notes (1, 3, 5, ♭7). It has a very 'rock and roll' sound to it. |

| mode name | Aeolian |
|---|---|
| formula | 1, 2, ♭3, 4, 5, ♭6, ♭7 |
| description | Sounds quite sad because it is exactly the same as the minor scale. Goes hand in hand with minor chords because it contains the 1, ♭3 and 5. |

| mode name | Locrian |
|---|---|
| formula | 1, ♭2, ♭3, 4, ♭5, ♭6, ♭7 |
| description | Has a certain impending doom sound to it. It relates well to diminished chords because it contains the 1, ♭3 and ♭5 notes used to build diminished chords. Diminished chords are the chords you hear played in black and white movies when someone is tied to the train tracks and a train is coming! |

Modes are named after Greek islands and people. Making up your own way of identifying the character and colour of each mode is a great way to remember them.

# CHEAT SHEET

This is the rote learning (memorisation by repetition) part of the book. I couldn't call myself a guitar teacher if I hadn't provided an explanation of *how* or *why* these scales work with 12 Bar Blues, but I also understand some people just want to play without getting too cerebral about it.

So for those who just want to dive in and improvise over the 12 Bar Blues in A, here is the information you need.

Use the A Mixolydian mode over the A7 chord:

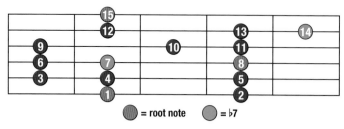

Use the A Dorian mode over the D7 or D9 chord:

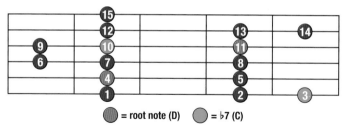

Use the A Ionian mode over the E7 or E9 chord:

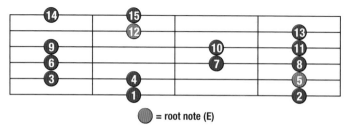

Try playing over just one chord at a time for a while so you get used to the mode shapes. Try to emphasise the root and ♭7 notes. Alternatively, you could use just the Mixolydian mode belonging to the root of each dom7 or 9th chord, for example, A Mixolydian over A7, D Mixolydian over D7, E Mixolydian over E7 and so on.

# WHAT ARE ARPEGGIOS?

The word 'arpeggio' comes from the Italian, meaning 'to spread a chord' – like how a harp is played.

On guitar, an arpeggio consists of notes from a chord played more like a scale; one note after the next either from the bottom upwards or the top downwards.

Consider that songs are made up of one or many 'chord progressions'. A chord progression is a series of chords that sound good together.

When improvising over a song made up of one or many chord progressions, playing the individual notes that make up the chords you are playing over will *always* sound correct. For this reason arpeggios are a great tool for any improviser's artillery ... and they sound cool.

# TWO MOVEABLE ARPEGGIO SHAPES FOR THE 12 BAR BLUES

As discussed, this section features the popular rock and blues chord progression, the 12 Bar Blues. Here are the arpeggios for the chords used in the 12 Bar Blues.

## Dominant 7th arpeggios

Position 1 (root note on the E string)

**Formula:** 1 3 5 ♭7

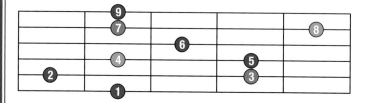

Position 2 (root note on the A string)

**Formula:** 1 3 5 ♭7

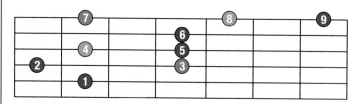

These arpeggios are moveable shapes, which means you can use them to play *every* dom7 arpeggio simply by moving them to the position on the neck relevant to the key you wish to play them in.

For example, if I wanted to play an Adom7 arpeggio, I would make the first note of the arpeggio shape I am playing an A. This could either be the 5th fret of the E string or the 12th fret of the A string depending on which arpeggio shape I want to play (position 1 or position 2).

Dominant 7th chords and arpeggios are also just referred to as 7th and Dom7th.

# USING ARPEGGIOS IMPROVISING OVER THE 12 BAR BLUES

Use the A7 arpeggio when the A7 chord is being played in the 12 Bar Blues:

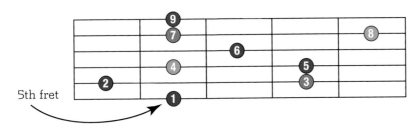

Use the D7 arpeggio when the D9 chord is being played in the 12 Bar Blues:

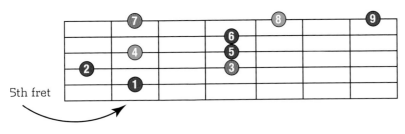

Use the E7 arpeggio when the E9 chord is being played in the 12 Bar Blues:

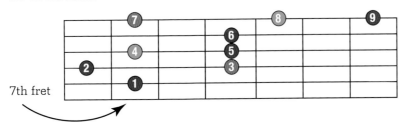

You can experiment with a combination of the modes we have learnt and these arpeggios. A good improviser often uses a combination of modes, licks and arpeggios.

# Playing Techniques

## HOW TO PRACTISE SCALES IN A USEFUL WAY FOR IMPROVISING

Knowing how to play your scales forwards and backwards doesn't always mean you will be able to improvise easily with them. Improvising is not usually executed in such a linear way and if you try to play like that, it will most likely sound as though you are playing up and down a scale as opposed to improvising. To improvise a melody that isn't simply the notes of the scale, you need to skip notes, repeat notes, skip strings, and add expression and rhythm etc.

A good way to practise your scales is to turn the linear motion I referred to on its head. Try to challenge your knowledge of the scale pattern.

On the following pages I will include examples of the following techniques: sequencing notes, sequencing notes using intervals, consistent speed exercises, bending notes, sliding notes, vibrato and using octaves.

# SEQUENCING NOTES

Sequencing means to arrange notes in a recurring, logical pattern. I will use the A major scale to demonstrate a typical sequencing pattern.

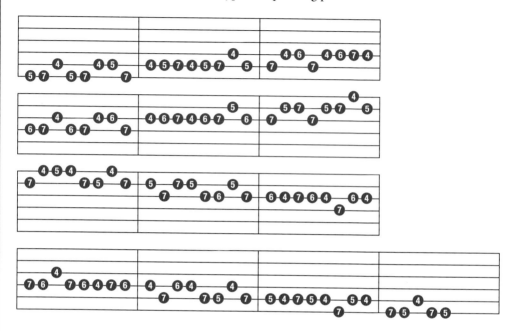

# SEQUENCING NOTES USING INTERVALS

Playing through a scale and moving up by 3rds, 4ths, 5ths or 6ths can create a cool melodic effect. Find the patterns I've created with these sequences and apply them to any scale. These examples are in the key of A major.

3rds

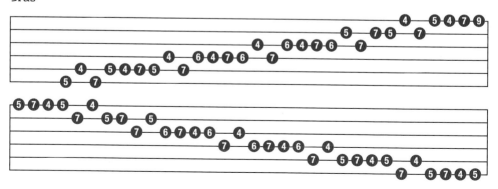

## 4ths

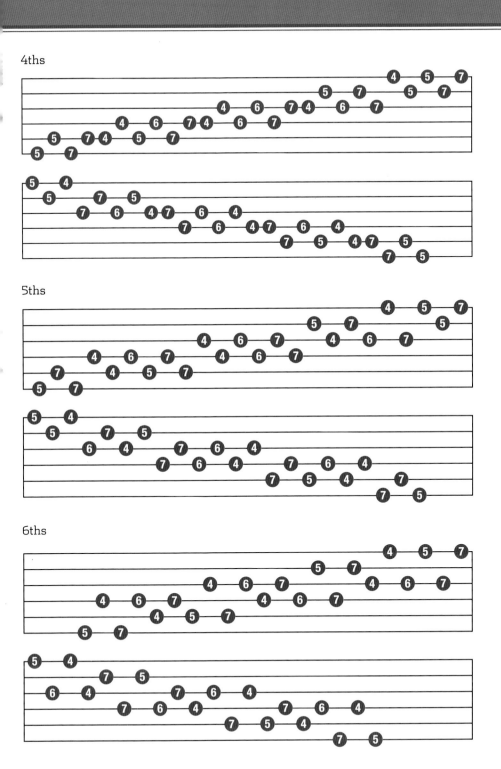

## 5ths

## 6ths

# CONSISTENT SPEED
# EXERCISES – RHYTHM

As mentioned at the beginning of this section, improvising is not just about knowing your scale notes forwards and backwards – a lot of other important elements come into play. One of those elements is rhythm.

The best way to become good at rhythm is to practise it! There are four main rhythm exercises I will show you to get you started using the major scale.

### Quarter notes

Each note is played on the count of 1, 2, 3, 4.

### Eighth notes

Each note is played on the count of 1 &, 2 &, 3 &, 4 &. (You play notes on the '&' also.)

### Sixteenth notes

Each note is played on the count of 1 e & a, 2 e & a, 3 e & a, 4 e & a. (You play notes on the 'e', '&' and 'a' also.)

Half an eighth is a sixteenth so the speed is exactly double of what it was with eighth notes.

### Triplets

Each note is played on the count of 1 & a, 2 & a, 3 & a, 4 & a. (You play notes on the '&' and 'a' also.)

Triplets are 3 notes in the time of 2. Tap your foot in the same constant beat as before '1, 2, 3, 4, 1, 2, 3, 4' and so on. Now while you tap your foot say the word TRIP-A-LET, broken up into 3 syllables in each beat like so:

| 1 | | | 2 | | | 3 | | | 4 | | |
|---|---|---|---|---|---|---|---|---|---|---|---|
| trip | a | let | trip | a | let | trip | a | let | trip | a | let |
| 1 | & | a | 2 | & | a | 3 | & | a | 4 | & | a |

It is a good idea to use a metronome to help you practise these rhythms with a solid reference for consistency. You can buy electric metronomes from any good music store or you can even download software metronomes from the internet.

# BENDING NOTES

Think of any rock guitar solo. That wailing sound is made by bending the strings or bending a single string. The idea is to push the string up on the guitar neck to raise the tension of the string, and this in turn raises the pitch. There is quite a degree of accuracy required to execute bending notes in a convincing way; that is, not sounding like a cat going crazy on the back fence.

There are two frequently used types of bends – 'half step' and 'whole step' bends. We learnt about half steps and whole steps on page 72.

### Bending

1. A good way to practise bending notes up a half step is to pick a note on the guitar, for example, the D note on the high E string (10th fret).

2. Now play the note a half step up (D♯ on the 11th fret).

3. Now return to the original note (D on the 10th) and bend the note until it reaches the same pitch as the D♯. You only pick the note once, then bend it up.

This will take a bit of practise to nail correctly.

Repeat this process when practising whole step bends, but replace the half step with a whole step.

# SLIDING NOTES

Slides are another cool-sounding technique for guitar playing and improvising.

1. Play the note on the 3rd fret high E string (G).

2. Now keep your finger down the whole time and slide it up to the 5th fret of the high E string without releasing any tension.

You should hear the note sliding 'up'. You can slide forwards and backwards and to any note from anywhere.

# VIBRATO

Vibrato is achieved on guitar in two main ways:

**1.** Up and down (a very subtle version of a half step bend).

**2.** Side to side (like a violinist)

The aim is to create a pulsating-type effect in the way a vocalist or cellist does. This adds a lot of dimension, expression and feeling to your playing.

# USING OCTAVES

I am going to show you six commonly used movable octave shapes. As learnt on page 81, an octave is the 8th note of a major scale played against or simultaneously with the 1st note of the major scale.

When played simultaneously on guitar, this creates a thick, cool sound, as made famous by Charlie Christian, George Benson and many guitarists after them.

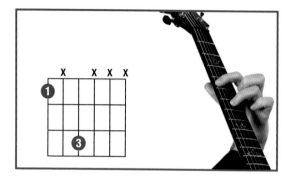

You can also use this shape on the A string.

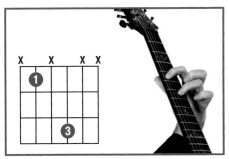

The shape changes when playing octaves on the D string.

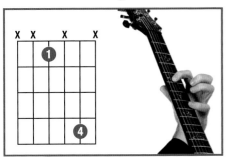

You can also use this shape on the G string.

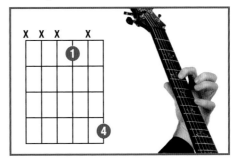

Then there are octave shapes using wider gaps between the strings.

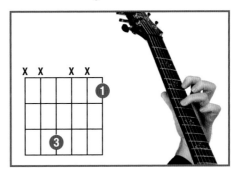

Here is the A major scale using these octave shapes:

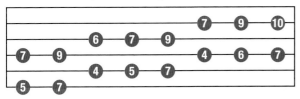

# CONCLUSION

Music is a bit like quantum mechanics; the more you know, the more you realise you don't know! I say this not to be discouraging, but to point out that to be a musician is to be a student in perpetuity.

When focusing on improvisation for beginners, there are really two main categories of guitarists:

1. Completely beginner guitarists who want to jump straight into improvisation.

2. Guitarists of varying levels who are beginners at improvisation.

This book is my attempt to provide information, instruction and answers for both profiles.

Improvising can be as simple as finger painting or as complex as an Escher drawing, so it was a challenge to identify what points to focus on. I sincerely hope this book has opened some doors for you and demystified some of that intimidating music theory that gets in the way of your progress.

Please drop into my website and stay posted for updates around some of the topics covered in this book: www.stevemackayguitar.com

Cheers,

Steve

# ABOUT THE AUTHOR

Steve MacKay is a highly accomplished musician, lead guitarist, music producer and guitar coach. He started playing guitar at age 8 and now regularly plays, writes and produces music with some of the biggest names in the music industry. He is also a skilled guitar teacher and a best-selling author of guitar tuition books and DVDs.

Steve has performed and recorded professionally in the USA, the UK, Europe and Australia, on high-profile radio and TV shows, on nationally televised music awards and on stage including accompanying Delta Goodrem on her promotional tours. He has also worked with international producers and songwriters, has written, produced and played on songs for Christine Anu, Delta Goodrem, Brian McFadden and Australian music legend Brian Cadd, and has recorded sessions for television and film programs including the Mighty Morphin' Power Rangers (Disney) and The Secret Life of Us.

As a teacher, Steve's most relevant skill is the ability to make it easy for others to learn what he knows. He demystifies the art of guitar performance into small chunks of information that are:

- Easy to understand;
- Easy to learn; and
- Easy to implement

His simplified teaching techniques have helped countless people learn to play the guitar with ease and enjoyment.

Steve would like to say, 'Thank you to the two most influential guitar teachers I have had: Tony Calabro and Samantha Rainy.'